THE LAW SCHOOL
DECISION GAME

THE LAW SCHOOL DECISION GAME

A PLAYBOOK FOR PROSPECTIVE LAWYERS

ANN K. LEVINE, ESQ.

Bestselling author of
The Law School Admission Game: Play Like An Expert
and the Law School Expert blog

The Law School Decision Game: A Playbook for Prospective Lawyers
By Ann K. Levine, Esq.

First edition copyright © 2011 Ann K. Levine

Library of Congress Control Number: 2011936178

ISBN: 978-0-9838453-0-0

Published by Abraham Publishing, Santa Barbara, CA

CONTENTS

PART IV: BUILDING YOUR CAREER IN LAW

To our grandmothers
For continuing to inspire us

Sylvia Good
Anna Kowel
Laura Kowel
Phyllis Levine
Madlyne Zoltan

ACKNOWLEDGMENTS

MY law school admission consulting clients inspired this book: so many bright people going into law, many of them asking difficult questions about the career that lies ahead of them. I especially want to thank my clients and former clients who took the time to review an early draft of this book and provide their feedback:

- Amanda El-Dakhakhni (Yale Law School class of 2014)
- Hagop Boyaci (University of California-Irvine School of Law class of 2014)
- Valentina Castillo (Georgetown University Law Center class of 2013)
- Brian Choc (University of California-Irvine School of Law class of 2014)
- Fawn Harringon (University of California-Hastings class of 2013)
- Elvira Kras, my research assistant for this book, whose wisdom and insight helped guide its focus (Columbia Law School class of 2014)
- Rebecca Sivitz (University of Pennsylvania School of Law class of 2012)
- Ethan Park (Stanford Law class of 2011).

I also relied upon the advice and assistance of colleagues,

several of whom took time to provide feedback and support. I highly recommend that all prospective lawyers follow them on Twitter: Amanda Ellis (@aellislegal), Jasper Kim (@jasperskim), Kevin Houchin (@kevinhouchin), Spencer Aronfeld (@aronfeld), and author Jenna McCarthy (@jennawrites) (who lives in my town and whom I actually hope to meet on purpose one day).

To gather the opinions of 300 lawyers, I needed help from my friends. Special thanks to my brother, Gene Kowel (for distributing the survey to his fanbase); Marni Lennon and Leo Chu (for introducing me to some of the people we interviewed for this book); and Charles Roboski, Assistant Dean for Admissions and Financial Aid, Michigan State University College of Law; Scott Carter; and Ernie Varela (for offering their insights on an early draft of the book). Thanks especially to my network of Facebook friends for being so responsive to all of my requests for quotes, connections, and title ideas. I also need to thank my brilliant and insightful editor (and aunt) Ruth Bloom.

In addition to my virtual colleagues, three hard-working, dynamic, forward-thinking, fun women have joined the LawSchoolExpert.com team; without them, I could not do everything that I do in my business and in my life:

Elizabeth Redman, my Marketing and Projects Manager (whose responsibility for this book and its success will come largely after it is published; I'm not sure how I did this without her on my first book, or how I managed the first five years of my business for that matter);

Jocelyn Glantz, Law School Admission Consultant (my East-Coast soul mate, whose early review of the book was a huge help and whose relationship with Law School Expert is a fabulous example of what can happen when you reach out to strangers with similar interests);

Kamila Storr, proofreader and editor (my good friend, who now has my back in all things related to knitting, editing, and Anglophile literature).

I also want to thank my family:

Haley and Nicole, who try not to bother mommy when she is working and who loved that I dedicated my last book to them (putting too much pressure on me to come up with something clever now that Haley's reading skills have surpassed "Dream Big. Do Good. Be True.");

Selma Burhan, who melds so beautifully into our family and without whom I would not be able to work and play tennis guilt-free;

Brent, whose support and encouragement make everything possible, and whose practice as a California Bar Certified Specialist in Workers Compensation has taught me more about the practice of law—and about business—than anything I learned in law school.

INTRODUCTION

INFORMATION is power. If you're thinking about going to law school, this book will give you the power to make good decisions about:

- Whether to attend law school;
- Which law school is right for you;
- What you can reasonably expect from a career in law;
- What kind of career you want; and
- How to build your career while still in law school.

To answer these questions, we went right to the source—we heard from more than 300 practicing lawyers.[1] As a law school admission consultant and law school advice blogger (www. LawSchoolExpert.com/blog), I know that people are confused and concerned about the current job market for lawyers and how this factors into their decisions about whether and where to attend law school. It is time to put real information in the hands of law school applicants.

Making Informed Decisions

More information leads to smarter decisions. This book is part of making a smart decision. It may talk you out of law

---

[1] 258 attorneys completed our survey. In addition, we interviewed approximately 50 attorneys we knew personally and who responded to HARO (Help a Reporter Out) requests. For more about who comprised the survey, see Chapter 2, entitled "300 Lawyers Walk into the Bar."

school, or it may solidify your decision to attend. In any case, learning what lawyers actually do, how they built their careers, and what they think about the choices they have made will help you decide what you want from your own life and career. I hope that their feedback will enable you to consider things you may not have thought much about at this point in your life, such as a career's impact on raising a family, how much money you really need to enjoy the life that you want, and how hard you are going to have to work to get there.

Once armed with this information, you'll be ready to make some big decisions. You will be equipped with real facts, not platitudes about law being a helping profession that requires analytical skills and interaction with people of various backgrounds. You will hear whether it really matters if you go to a top law school, how much the cost of law school should factor into your decision, what you should be doing during law school to have a job when you get out, and when and how to create an area of specialization in law. You will learn about the many different ways a law degree can be put to use, and why others have chosen to walk away from a career in law and how they did it.

You already know that attending law school is not a decision to be taken lightly. If you end up choosing law school because your parents feel better telling their friends that you're in law school than sleeping on their couch and scooping ice cream for a living, then you'll be unmotivated in law school and you'll end up right back on the couch after graduation (with the extra benefit of student loan debt). If you've been out in the working world for a while and you're looking for a career change, you may be considering the merits of a JD versus an MBA. Whether you're in either of these groups or somewhere in the middle, you will benefit from taking the time to read this book: it will give you an honest glimpse into the varied lives of different kinds of lawyers.

After all, choosing to get a law degree is only the first step: next you'll need to decide where you want to live and which areas of law are good fits for your skills and personality traits. Leonard Stone, a plaintiff-side personal injury partner in the Las Vegas firm Shook & Stone, said it best: "When someone tells me they want to be a lawyer, I want to know what they mean by that." After all, what he does is much different than what an in-house corporate counsel does (like Noah Solomon, whom you'll hear more from in Chapter 16). Leonard has people crying in his office and works on a feast-or-famine contingency fee basis. Noah deals with businesses and their decision makers as a contract attorney in the field of entertainment law. Leonard worries about paying the overhead and hiring employees and partnership agreements while Noah has coffee provided for him but a boss to answer to. These are just some of this book's examples demonstrating that there is no cookie-cutter mold of who a lawyer is, what a lawyer does, how much a lawyer makes, or what quality of life a lawyer leads.

Career Satisfaction: Oxymoron?

The point of this book is to illuminate some of the benefits and detriments of the legal profession generally, and certain areas of law specifically, so that you can make a wise decision about whether this is a career choice that will make you happy with your life, and whether you feel drawn to one type of practice over another. We also give you advice on how to figure those answers out beyond this book because we want you to avoid being miserable with your career and life choices. I went to law school because I saw it as a career choice (or springboard) that would help me create the life I wanted for myself. This holds true today for me, for my husband, and for many lawyers that I know. However, it's evident from reading blogs and discussion forums that not everyone feels as we do.

Therefore, we can assume that there must be a disconnect that occurs between the moment that people decided to attend law school and the moment in their legal careers when they decide they are not happy. What people ***thought*** would make them happy in their careers must have been what they ***thought*** they would find in the legal profession. Were unhappy lawyers wrong about what would make them happy? Were they wrong about the legal profession? Would they be equally unhappy in any job? Or did they just not do their research before applying to law school? Many lawyers shared with us that law school was a "default" decision made because it seemed impressive and productive. Are they more or less likely to be happy with their choice? By sharing their responses and synthesizing them, I hope to diminish the possibility that you will join the ranks of the "unhappy."

In addition to surveying lawyers, we surveyed 100 people who are currently applying to law school and planning to enroll this fall or next. We wanted to know their reasons for entering the profession, their expectations, and their varied approaches in making their law school and career decisions. I did this because, as a law school admission consultant, I wanted to see if the messages from the media were getting through or paralyzing the decision-making process. Are people thinking more seriously about whether they really want to be lawyers? Are they considering what student loan debt would mean for their future lives?

Understanding the Job Market

Two years ago, applications to law school jumped as the economy tanked. I saw that people were hoping to ride out the recession in school, hoping to emerge with a JD degree in a brighter world. What we are seeing is that the turnaround is not coming as quickly as we thought, and I wanted to see what current applicants could learn from people who are out there in the field and who have been living with JD degrees for a number of years.

Through the survey and through interviews by phone and e-mail, we learned how smart lawyers built their careers in extremely diverse fields (entertainment law, international law, commercial litigation, public interest advocacy, family law, alternative legal careers, and more). You will gain insights into how their choice of law school and choice of activities during law school helped them build their careers. And, you will benefit from their candid responses about whether and how they would do it all over again if they could.

One of our respondents stated this book's purpose perfectly: an assistant district attorney who attended Fordham Law advises law school applicants to "know the realities of practicing law and go into law school with their eyes wide open before accumulating $150k+ debt." Her purpose is also my purpose, and it has two parts. The first part is learning the realities of practicing law, and the second part is deciding whether to take on debt at a higher ranking school or taking a scholarship to another law school instead. Through the information gathered in this book, I hope to guide you in making both of these decisions.

Choosing a Law School

After learning through this book how different kinds of lawyers spend their days, and once you decide that one or more of these lawyers' lives would work for you, you have a more immediate decision: where to attend law school. It would be somewhat easier if everyone who wanted to practice international law went to School A, entertainment law hopefuls went to School B, and intellectual property law specialists went to School C; however, you'd then face the problem of being pigeonholed and trapped into a field of law you might later discover to be a terrible fit for you. This is what makes it so easy to fall back on how law schools are ranked when choosing a law school: it removes the burden from you to do research, visit the schools, talk to students and alumni, and investigate the cost of attendance. Certainly, if the rankings say School D is better than School E, then what decision could there possibly be for you to make?

As it turns out, law school rankings do not tell the whole story. A law school's ranking does not take into account the success of its graduates or the level of satisfaction they feel in their careers. By talking to lawyers, seeing what they've achieved, and finding out how they got there, we saw that most lawyers feel they could have gone to a lesser-ranked law school and had the same career; yet, people who went to Top 5 law schools swear that it opened doors for them. Then there are the examples that show otherwise: my husband is a partner in a law firm where the attorneys went to Georgetown, Loyola-Los Angeles, University of Miami, California Western, and state bar-accredited schools. Guess what? They are all doing the same job every day, working with the same kinds of clients, handling the same level of work, negotiating the same kinds of deals, doing the same kinds of trials, and being paid according to the same scale. There is an old joke: "what do you call the guy who graduates last in his law school class? A lawyer."[2] For those of you who decide you are ready to apply to law school, information like this may help you choose which law school to attend because you will see where different attorneys have ended up and where they went to law school. You will learn about attorneys who went to Yale, Harvard, Stanford, Columbia, and NYU, as well as those who went to state bar-accredited schools and everywhere in between. You will also learn how to best use your time during law school to set yourself up to become a successful (and employed) lawyer.

What You're Getting Yourself Into

Together with Elvira Kras, a student at Columbia Law, I have surveyed and interviewed approximately 300 attorneys nationwide, at all stages of their careers (legal and otherwise). In approaching this endeavor, we wanted to know what lawyers actually do on a daily basis, what their lives are like, how they feel about their chosen profession, and what doors are really open to those with a law degree who decide not to practice law. We wanted to see if there were correlations between types of law practiced, hours worked, money made, and satisfaction in career, family, and personal life. We wanted to see whether attorneys who attended top law schools had "impressive" jobs and attorneys who attended regional law schools had less glamorous jobs.[3] We asked them how they got those jobs and

---

[2] Of course, he can only give legal advice if he passes the bar, but all he has to do is pass—not get the highest score.

[3] Instead of using the terminology provided by *U.S. News and World Report* to refer to Tier 3 or Tier 4 or "bottom 100" schools, I call them "regional" law schools because it is the intent of most of these law schools to serve the local population and provide lawyers for their communities. As a result, these law schools are at a huge disadvantage in popular ranking methodologies because a judge or law professor in Wyoming may not be familiar with a law school in Massachusetts and vice versa when asked

gathered information to help you make yourself more market-able as a prospective attorney.

Most of all, however, we wanted to gather and synthesize enough information to help you, the potential law student, decide whether this really is a profession you want to enter. Explore whether you are well-suited for it, and whether you are prepared to do what it takes to create a career trajectory that will still make you happy 20 years from now.

The key question is: ***if given the opportunity to do it all over again, would they?*** The responses will enlighten you, surprise you, and help you make decisions that are right for your life, based on credible, helpful, real anecdotes and opin-ions of lawyers who have been out in the real world using their law degrees in both traditional and nontraditional occupations.

> As the student speaker at my law school graduation in 1999, I quoted a cartoon I'd read: "Why do we want the moments of our lives to pass so quickly but the whole thing to last forever?" How you spend your career **is** really how you spend your life. Before you choose it, be sure of it. We hope every page of this book will lead you to make decisions that are right for you.

Economics Changes Everything

If I'd written this book in 2010, I'd be starting with the fact that law school applications were at an all-time high: schools including Cornell, in the winter wasteland of Ithaca, New York, were reporting increases of up to 70 percent in applications

---

to judge a school's reputation, among other factors (including the quality of educa-tion available), in one state's public university system over another's when evaluating candidates.

received. Compared to the previous decade, law school enrollment was up 19 percent.[4]

In that environment, this book would be vital: certainly, all of those people suffering from a deserted post-college job market and laid-off employees seeking career changes couldn't have been absolutely sure they wanted to be lawyers. This book would have helped them come to that realization and change their plans. Many of them did that even without this book.

As I write this book in 2011, the *Wall Street Journal* has reported a 12 percent decrease in law school applications for the fall 2011 entering class[5] (this isn't the first time law school applications have decreased significantly over a year's time; for example, the *New York Times* reported a 10 percent decrease in 2006[6]).The *Wall Street Journal* Law Blog asks, "Is Law School Losing Its Mojo?"[7] If the application slide was simply a decrease over one year (comparing it to the most competitive year ever for law school admission), it would hardly be noteworthy. However, application numbers are the lowest in 10 years.

What happened? People started talking about two things: debt and the job market. Everyone is talking about debt—it's a major political theme and it has trickled down to individuals. People are saving more and spending less.[8] Regarding law school debt specifically, all kinds of national news outlets and blogs are

---

[4] http://blogs.forbes.com/kurtbadenhausen/2011/03/08/
the-best-law-schools-for-getting-rich/.

[5] "Law School Loses Its Allure as Firm Jobs Are Scarce," http://online.
wsj.com/article/SB10001424052748704396504576204692878631986.
html?mod=WSJ_hp_MIDDLENexttoWhatsNewsThird.

[6] www.nytimes.com/2006/02/09/national/09law.html?scp=3&sq=law%20school%20
applications&st=Search.

[7] http://blogs.wsj.com/law/2011/02/09/is-law-school-losing-its-mojo/.

[8] www.wisebread.com/the-new-frugality-consume-less-save-more-live-better.

talking about the rise in law school tuition and the amount of debt people are taking on to go to law school. This topic is especially volatile in the context of the current legal job market. Recent law school graduates are, on the whole, struggling to find meaningful work, and the jobs they hoped to attain at prominent national law firms have largely dried up. Of course, those were the jobs people were chasing when they turned down scholarships to Top 30 schools to attend Top 15 schools because they wanted access to the large law firms (hereinafter referred to as BigLaw). BigLaw is tempting: it offers the best pay, sophisticated clients, and opens doors to other opportunities. But you can't count on it being an option for you because of changes in the marketplace. (For more about changes to the BigLaw community, see Chapter 11.) It's important to keep this in mind when taking on debt.

> There is a lot of buzz about the cost of law school, the debt people take on to attend, and the difficulty recent graduates are facing paying off their loans. Even the American Bar Association (ABA)—the agency that accredits law schools and oversees the legal profession—admits that "[t]he combination of the rising cost of a legal education and the realities of the job market mean that going to law school may not pay off for a large number of law students."[9]

When I first engage in consultation with my clients, I ask them whether the cost of tuition is an issue for them. It changes the advice I give them about where to apply to law school. The

---

[9] www.americanbar.org/groups/legal_education/resources/pre_law.html. (I actually wanted to include the entire three-page article as an appendix to this book, but the ABA would only allow me to include the URL: It's a must-read for law school applicants.)

fact is that some people have saved money for law school, plan to live at home, will attend public school, or choose a law school based on a scholarship. The debt issue doesn't apply equally to everyone. In *The $100,000 Gamble: Should I Go to Law School* (New York: R + S Media, 2011), Derek Roberti, PhD, Esq., provides a thorough economic analysis of attending law school and goes a step further by helping you decide whether law school is right for your personality and your aspirations.

Not everyone will encourage your idea to become a lawyer. One reason is financial, but another is general resentment toward lawyers, especially in the midst of financial scandals where lawyers are seen representing those accused of fraud and other misdeeds. I mean, lawyers are terrible people, aren't they? If not morally compromised, then they must be terribly unhappy, right? Everyone has these stories to share: "I knew a lawyer who was so crooked he…." Or "My aunt was a lawyer, but it made her completely miserable; she never got married and she had a heart attack by age 45." Statistics show that one in every four or five lawyers is addicted to the use of alcohol. *Best Practices for Legal Education* states, "It is well known that lawyers suffer higher rates of depression, anxiety, and other mental illness, suicide, divorce, alcoholism and drug abuse, and poor physical health than the general population or other occupations."[10]

Based on all of this, I'm sure people are asking you—and you are asking yourself—why on earth are you thinking about going to law school? If you read the *Wall Street Journal*, the *Washington Post*,[11] the *New York Times*, or blogs like Above the

---

[10] Roy Stuckey, *Best Practices for Legal Education: A Vision and a Roadmap* (Martell, CA: CLEA, 2007), 30.

[11] www.washingtonpost.com/wp-dyn/content/article/2010/10/30/
AR2010103000211.html.

Law, you would never in your right mind attend law school. The *New Republic* estimates that fewer than 45 percent of recent law graduates are in permanent legal positions.[12] According to these sources, there are no jobs, and what jobs do exist are only for those who attend Harvard, Yale, Stanford, or Columbia. As I told *U.S. News*,[13] the reason applications are down is that there is a lot of press about the job market for recent law school graduates. Our survey of prospective law students confirms this: of those who are unsure whether they will attend law school, 44 percent cite news articles about the legal job market as the reason for their hesitation.

There are a lot of disgruntled lawyers out there, and they are loud. They are blogging, tweeting, and screaming at the top of their lungs to dissuade you from going to law school. As a law school admission consultant, I urge people to thoroughly research law schools and the legal profession before enrolling; this is the best preventative medicine to keep you from becoming the person who trolls forums complaining about his or her chosen profession. After reading this book, if you decide to go to law school, you will go in with your eyes open, ready to take advantage of the opportunities offered, and prepared to build your own career rather than expecting someone to hand you a six-figure salary along with your JD degree.

My Point of View

I am proud to be a lawyer. I am very proud to be married to

[12] www.tnr.com/article/87251/law-school-employment-harvard-yale-georgetown.

[13] www.usnews.com/education/best-graduate-schools/top-law-schools/articles/2011/03/18/law-school-applications-take-a-dip; www.usnews.com/education/best-graduate-schools/top-law-schools/applying/articles/2010/07/14/as-law-school-tuitions-climb-so-does-demand.

a lawyer. In fact, I surround myself with lawyers: my brother, my father-in-law, my sister-in-law, four of our mutual cousins, and most of our friends are lawyers. Of my 1,000 Facebook friends, probably 700 are either lawyers or on their way to becoming lawyers. They are a diverse, interesting, inspirational, and—overall—happy bunch. As far as I know, none of my friends secretly wish they'd done something else. We are all very happy with the path we've chosen and the lives we lead, no matter how unsure we were of our decisions when we made them.

After graduating from the University of Miami with a Bachelor of Science in Communication, I took a job in advertising and went to the University of Miami School of Law at night, hedging my bets about which career might be better suited to me. I had a close friend, Steven E. Cohen, who was a 3L at University of Miami Law and whom I admired greatly. He told me that there was a prestige to law that few other professions offered, and he convinced me I'd be good at it so I followed in his footsteps. After my first-semester grades confirmed his suspicions, my decision was easy. I started attending full time and graduated magna cum laude in 1999 as a member of the Order of the Coif.

I thought I wanted to go to law school to be a civil rights attorney, and you'll read more about this in Chapter 3, but I felt a lot of pressure to go for jobs that weren't good fits for my personality and passions. At the same time, I was very involved on campus as a student leader, and the system of higher education was something about which I was both passionate and knowledgeable. I pretty much grew up on college campuses as my father rose through the ranks of college administration to become a dean during my formative years.

Even in college and law school, I was inclined to work

closely with the administration on orientation, student bar association activities, and other projects. Therefore, right out of law school, I took a job as Director of Student Services at the University of Denver College of Law. From there, I became Director of Admissions at California Western School of Law in San Diego, California (a fabulous example of the merits of a regional law school for the right candidate, as my husband is a successful graduate), and then at Loyola Law School in Los Angeles. During that time, I seated the entering classes; recruited applicants; decided whom to admit, whom to wait-list, whom to reject; and decided who would get scholarships. I reviewed thousands of law school applications and recommended and took action on those applications.

In 2004, I started LawSchoolExpert.com, a nationwide (and now worldwide) law school admission consulting company. We have since helped approximately 2,000 applicants through personalized consulting and thousands more through the blog and through my law school guidebook published in 2009. As part of this, I inevitably tell people when I think they should reconsider their plans, for example, when their credentials will preclude them from attaining their goals.[14]

I began *The Law School Admission Game: Play Like an Expert* by alerting the reader to my personal biases. Many of them dealt specifically with my experience getting people into law school, but some remain applicable for this book, including (in no particular order):

- I believe in the value of a "Fourth Tier" or "Regional Law School" education for the right person. I am not a school snob. Top law schools are great for some

---

[14] During a free initial consultation prior to signing up and through comments on my blog posts.

candidates, and regional law schools are great for other candidates.

- I feel strongly that law school applicants must understand that jobs are not handed out along with diplomas for most law school graduates. You must expect to hustle, work hard, and build your own bridges to your career goals.

- I do not consider it my job to convince anyone whether law school is the right decision. You must do your own research into the profession and think about your goals and aspirations. . . [I]t's a decision you should not take lightly.[15]

In addition to these disclosures, I would add the following:

- For those of you who have been following my blog, you know that I generally take a positive outlook on things. I am a lawyer (in an alternative legal career, something I devote an entire chapter to in this book [see Chapter 14]), and I am married to a lawyer (a partner in a six-office law firm). We are both happy that we went to law school; we feel that we grew personally and professionally as a result of attending law school. Additionally, we feel that attaining a law degree has allowed us to live a very nice life and support our family.

- I believe "good things happen to those who wait, but only what's left by those who hustle" (my favorite quote, by Abraham Lincoln). This is true of getting into law school, getting in from a waiting list, dealing with how hard you have to work while in law school,

---

[15] Ann K. Levine, *The Law School Admission Game: Play Like an Expert* (Santa Barbara, CA: Abraham Publishing, 2009), 14–16.

and doing what's necessary to be suitably employed after law school.

- I believe that current trends are just that—current—and that things will change, although they won't necessarily go back to the way they used to be. In my first draft of this book, I wrote that I believe that the structure of law firms will be slow to change—the billable hour is here to stay. However, some of the people I interviewed, who are far more intimately involved with these issues than I am, have almost convinced me otherwise.

- I believe that one way to a productive, lucrative career that allows lawyers more flexibility and balance in their lives is self-employment. As a result, I think law students should learn to think like entrepreneurs whether or not they go to work for a firm or go to work for themselves because—honestly, and as you will learn through reading this book—working for a firm really *is* working for yourself and a law degree may not offer *job security*, but it does offer *profession security*. No one can take away your bar license (except you, by bad behavior). You may lose a job, but you will have a way to employ yourself because you can always practice law.

I hope that my perspective and experience, along with that of the 300 attorneys who helped me with this endeavor, will help you to make the right decision about whether to go to law school.

PART I

DOING YOUR RESEARCH

"The vast majority of lawyering is drudgery work—it's sitting in a library, it's banging out a brief, it's talking to clients for endless hours."

—Sonia Sotomayor, Associate Justice of the Supreme Court of the United States

CHAPTER 1

BEING UNDECIDED

I T'S entirely possible to have too many choices in life. Research shows that the more choices we have, the harder time we have deciding between them. "[W]hen there is too much to choose from, we're unlikely to choose at all."[16] In the first chapter of *Undecided,* the authors share a story about a young woman who couldn't decide whether to attend business school or law school and was driven so crazy by indecision that she actually expressed a desire that her entire life be decided for her.

Law school is never the only option for anyone's career. Most of us could be perfectly happy doing something other than what we are doing. It's a question of whether you could be happier, and that very question drives people—especially college students and recent college graduates—insane. You're told that the world is your oyster; you could do anything you set your mind to doing. With that advice comes an enormous amount of pressure to pick something and excel at it, and excel at it very quickly. It's a common phenomenon, and one that is coined as a "quarter-life crises" with books and career counselors trying to

---

[16] Barbara Kelley and Shannon Kelley, *Undecided: How to Ditch the Endless Quest for Perfect and Find the Career—and Life—That's Right for You* (Berkeley, CA: Seal Press, 2011), 81.

reach people in their mid-to-late twenties and early thirties who don't know what to do next: law school, MBA programs, travel, or volunteer work, and who struggle with jobs that bore them and aren't as glamorous or important as what they expected for themselves (even if those expectations were based on fallacy).

How do you know if you're lacking direction or just indecisive? Does law school sound important? (As in, "Hi, nice to meet you. Oh, me? I'm in law school.") Are you going to law school to impress parents, peers, ex-boyfriends or ex-girlfriends, people from high school who made fun of you, or other people who didn't believe in you? If so, then when does this game end? Are you not good enough unless you go to a Top 10 school? Are you not good enough unless you work for a big firm in a big city? Drive a fancy car? Wear designer clothes? Have the world's biggest house? If you're reading this book, you're at a point in your life when you can stop the madness and think about what you really want from life.

Do you want a challenge? Do you want a job that makes you think? Do you want to interact with people and coach them through some of the most stressful personal and business decisions of their lives? Do you want your kids to see that you work hard for everything they have? Do you like to read? Do you write clearly and fairly easily? Are you good with deadlines? Do you like to multitask? Do you (admit it!) feed off of stress and craziness a little bit? Do you like to give advice to your friends and family members? If so, a career in law may be your perfect match.

> Money, status, or inertia are not those reasons because they won't make it all worth it in the end. Most people enter law school with hopes of "helping people." The opposite was true for me: I didn't grow up with much

and I wanted to provide for my family in the long run. In short, it was the money. But now, becoming a lawyer is meaningful because it is also about using what I know to make life better for someone else. Before becoming a lawyer, my only advice is this: Understand why you're doing it, be thoughtful and listen to yourself.[17]

You need to make the right decision *for you.* There is no one right answer to tell you whether to go to law school or walk away, and certainly each person can enjoy more than one kind of career.[18] It's ok not to be absolutely certain that a life in law is the only life for you. However, unless someone else is paying for law school, you need to be pretty convinced that you could be successful and happy as a lawyer before you invest three years and a lot of money. This is obviously a question people are taking more seriously: in our poll, fewer than half of the individuals planning to apply to law school in the next year say they "will absolutely attend."

Many of the attorneys we surveyed advised prospective law students to work in the legal field before committing to attend law school. We asked 100 prospective and current law school applicants about their current level of familiarity with the legal profession, and what we found is illustrated in Figure 1.1.

---

[17] Kate Rykken, "Becoming a Lawyer: The Prize for Eating All Your Pie Is More Pie," *Cornell Sun*, April 23, 2009.

[18] I could have remained a Director of Admissions, or gotten my PhD in Higher Education, continued my work as a litigator, or become a rabbi—all of which were options I seriously considered and which I believe I would be relatively happy and successful doing. But I am also the kind of person who (1) believes that whatever I am doing is the best possible thing, and (2) if I don't feel that way, I take swift and decisive action to change court and find the best possible thing.

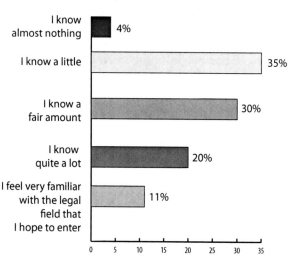

Figure 1.1 **How familiar do you believe you are with the practice of the law?**

I think we can all agree that it's a smart idea to know something about what you're getting yourself into. Here is what some attorneys had to say about gaining familiarity with the practice of law before attending law school:

- A recent graduate of Arizona State says people should go to law school "if they earnestly want to be a lawyer and have some real world experience with what lawyers actually do, then there is only one way to be a lawyer and they must go to law school." He urges people who do not know what lawyers do *on a daily basis* to work or volunteer in a law office.

- One senior associate who bills between 2,000 to 2,500 hours per year said, "I would not encourage someone to attend law school unless they had some exposure, either by knowing attorneys or by working in a firm environment, to the demands of a legal career. It's not an easy job."

- Jeralyn Cox Ehlers graduated from the University of San Diego School of Law[19] and advises those considering law school to work in a law office, not just to help their career choices about whether to practice law and what areas of law appeal to them, but also because it will improve your job prospects if you do decide to enter the legal field.

> I started working in law offices when I was only 18. I have been a file clerk, runner, receptionist, legal secretary, paralegal, law clerk (unpaid), law clerk (paid), associate attorney, and I am now a partner of my own practice. My work before law school helped me when it was time to find a job, as I had connections and a skill set which set me apart from other applicants. I was one of the few people in my graduating class to have a job secured before the start of my third year.

- Carly Slack Anderson, a graduate of the University of Texas, gives similar advice. "I'd advise them to work at a firm for a year if possible before starting law school. I wish I would have done that. One of our employees just graduated college and decided to work here for a year before law school. A little over halfway through the year, she decided that it wasn't for her."
- Assistant Dean of Loyola University Chicago School of Law Marianne Deagle actually encourages people

---

[19] Throughout the book, references to universities are to law schools unless specifically referenced otherwise.

to work three to five years before going to law school. In fact, 30 percent of respondents said that work in a law firm prior to attending law school is one of the experiences that assisted them in their current career.

• Amanda Ellis, author of *The 6Ps of the BIG 3™ for Job-Seeking JDs* (Dallas, TX: Something Different Publishing, 2010), told me that "students should try to work in a variety of firms, if possible, since the type of practice can attract someone to the legal field (or push them away). For example, a firm that does 100 percent insurance defense work may scare off someone who would love tax law."

Of course, the work you would be doing working for a law firm as a clerk or paralegal is not lawyer work, but—if you use your time wisely—you will gain exposure to lawyers and what they do to determine whether you could see yourself doing something similar.[20] Another reason to work in a legal field is that if you do decide to go to law school there may be a job for you upon graduation. For example, my husband's firm just hired its former file clerk as an attorney!

To really find out what a lawyer does, you absolutely must talk to at least three lawyers. Here are some ideas about how to meet them:

1. Ask your parents to introduce you to their friends who are lawyers and/or to their personal or business lawyers. Talk to these lawyers about what they do.

---

[20] In *The Law School Admission Game: Play Like an Expert*, I advised applicants not to go out and work for a law firm just to boost their resumes. I still stand by this advice, but I've adjusted my views somewhat based on the legal marketplace and conversations I've had with so many lawyers about the importance of building connections with lawyers early in your career.

2. Ask around at your religious or cultural organizations to see if there are any lawyers you could talk to.

3. Check with the career services professionals at your college or local law school to see if they can introduce you to any lawyers.

4. Check the state bar website for attorneys in your area.

5. Attend an event that lawyers are likely to attend, perhaps at a law school.

If you are unwilling to do this, or just have decided right here and now that there is no way you are going to do this, then you've made your career decision. If you're not curious about what lawyers do and/or you don't feel comfortable taking the initiative reaching out, and/or you are too lazy to spend the time to do so, then law school and a career in law are not for you. On the other hand, if you are willing to engage lawyers in conversation, shadow them on one of their daily journeys, and still think this may be what you are looking for, continue reading.

CHAPTER 2

300 LAWYERS WALK
INTO THE BAR

PRIOR to sending out the survey, I envisioned one of two possible outcomes: (1) it would confirm that people feel gratified in their profession as a lawyer over the long term and that they felt able to support their families and lifestyles doing meaningful—if demanding—work, or (2) people would almost universally regret their career choices and publishing the results would pretty much drive me out of business as a law school admission consultant. I hoped for the first and feared the second. I expected that a large number of recent law school graduates regret attending law school, but was surprised at how many people there are who make a lot of money *and* have time to spend with their families yet would advise other people not to attend law school. What's up with that? (I promise, we'll explore it.)

Who did we send the survey to? Admittedly, there was a West Coast/East Coast bias because that's where most of my personal contacts are; however, I tried to make up for that by specifically reaching out via Twitter, Facebook, HARO, and bloggers to people in the middle of the country. I attended a conference with lawyers from across the country and was able to fill out some spots by procuring the involvement of those in attendance. And, although I feared that there would be an over-whelming number of responses by my former classmates at the University of Miami School of Law, it actually turns out that (1) most of the University of Miami graduates who participated graduated long before I did and I have no idea how they found out about the survey, and (2) my social networking contacts—people I only met through Twitter before they became Facebook friends and trusted colleagues and mentors—helped me cover places in between (like Texas, which had a big following).

I purposely did not reach out to an overabundance of lawyers who graduated within the last five years because of the extreme nature of the recent job market. I didn't want these responses to overwhelm a survey meant to capture the entirety of the legal profession, especially because I (correctly) predicted that these attorneys would be overwhelmingly negative about their decisions since they would have entered law school when the job market was good and left it when it was at its worst. I operate under the assumption that the current economy—a reality that must be faced—is not permanent, and although there will be changes in the way law is practiced (perhaps!), the world will still need lawyers (just as it always has).

I elected not to ask people about specific salary ranges because I felt it would deter people from responding (especially people who know me personally and wouldn't want me seeing that information). Therefore, I took a number reported to be the median salary for all lawyers nationwide and asked people whether they made "significantly less," "slightly less," "about the same," "slightly more," or "significantly more."[21] Because

---

[21] I used $105,000 as the number on the survey and asked respondents to assume it

it's true that these responses are difficult to quantify, I have outside data to help illustrate the pay issue.

As an incentive to participate, I told people they would be performing a good deed, helping people decide whether and/or where to attend law school and what to expect from the legal profession. I told them the survey would take 5 to 10 minutes to complete and participants would be entered to win a $100 gift card for Amazon.

What did I hope to find? That, overall, people with law degrees felt:

- They had opportunities they would not have had otherwise.
- They made good livings, especially in 10 to 20 years after law school graduation.
- They probably didn't need to attend highly ranked law schools to achieve what they have achieved.
- They wish they'd paid more attention to the cost of law school instead of the brand name of the school.
- Law is hard work and not glamorous.
- Key factors in success in any field are business skills and people skills.
- Most people who started at big firms left them.
- Most job opportunities are found through networking.

In the end, I'm pleased to report that my hopes were justified and my fears were not (at least not *yet*—anything can happen once the book is published!). My research assistant

---

was the median. Since then, I have found more reliable sources showing the median to be $113,000. Therefore, there might be a slight variance in the outcome where $7,000 would've made the difference between someone claiming they make "about the same" or "slightly more" than my median number of $105,000.

Elvira and I got to talk to a lot of really interesting lawyers who do fascinating things and who enjoy their lives and their livelihoods. We learned a lot from them, and we are excited to share their stories and advice with you.

You'll be tempted, perhaps, to skip over the graphs, tables, and numbers. In fact, you may feel your eyes gloss over and you may be thinking, "Is she kidding me with these statistics? If I wanted math, I would go to medical school or business school." However, understanding facts and knowing what to do with them—how to use and interpret them—is a skill that will carry you far on the LSAT, in law school, and in your career. So, be sure to read the graphs and tables.[22]

---

[22] That being said, I am not a statistician and my research was not done or checked by any scientific methods or experts. I apologize in advance if any of you PhDs considering law school (or people with 99th percentile LSAT scores) notice flaws in my question structures or assumptions.

Overview of Survey Responses

Figure 2.1 represents the approximate *U.S. News and World Report* rankings of our survey participants.

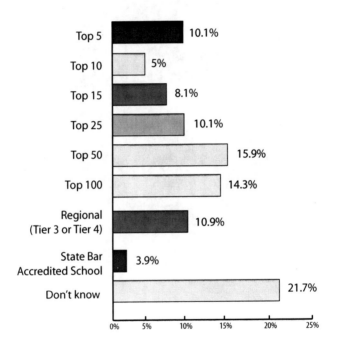

Figure 2.1 **At the time you attended, how was your law school ranked by *U.S. News and World Report*?**

- Top 5 — 10.1%
- Top 10 — 5%
- Top 15 — 8.1%
- Top 25 — 10.1%
- Top 50 — 15.9%
- Top 100 — 14.3%
- Regional (Tier 3 or Tier 4) — 10.9%
- State Bar Accredited School — 3.9%
- Don't know — 21.7%

Figure 2.2 shows that the majority of survey respondents currently practice law.

Figure 2.2 **Do you currently practice law?**

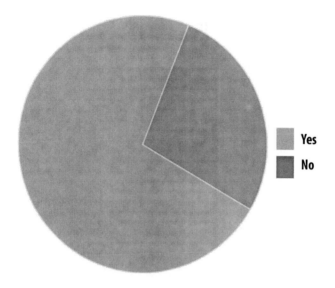

Yes

No

Figure 2.3 shows that respondents ranged from recent graduates to those with almost 50 years of experience as attorneys:

- 131 respondents graduated more than 11 years ago (41 of them have survived more than 20 years since graduating from law school),
- 61 had been in practice between 6 and 10 years,
- 60 were "Baby Lawyers" within 5 years of law school graduation.

Figure 2.3 **How many years since law school graduation?**

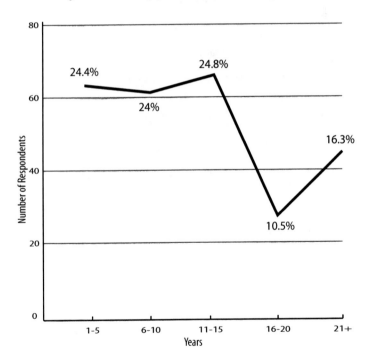

Figure 2.4 illustrates responses from lawyers at different phases of their careers.

Figure 2.4 **How would you describe the present phase of your career?**

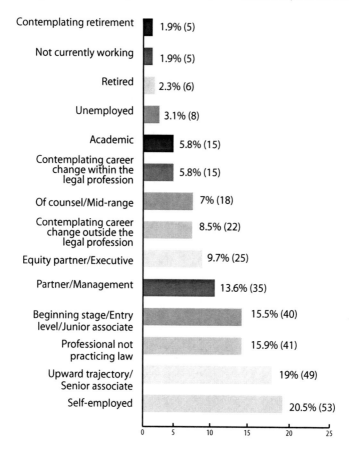

In Figure 2.5, we see a wide range of employers represented.[23]

Figure 2.5 **How would you characterize your current employer?**

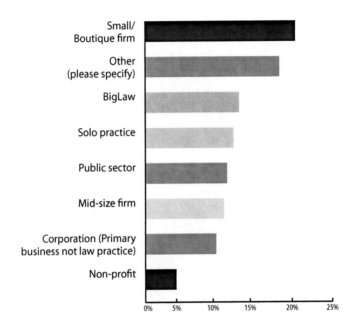

Figure 2.6 reflects the wide range of salaries earned by lawyers.

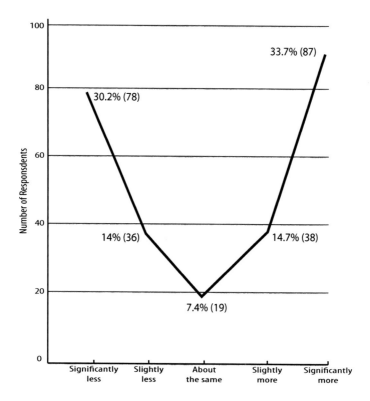

Figure 2.6 **Assuming the median attorney salary is $105,000, how much do you currently make?**

> By taking the time to understand the diversity of our survey respondents, you will be better able to appreciate the perspectives they share throughout the book about their employers, salaries, and law school choices.

PART II

IS LAW SCHOOL RIGHT FOR YOU?

"My parents wanted me to be a lawyer. But I don't think I would have been very happy. I'd be in front of the jury singing."

—Jennifer Lopez, singer and actress

CHAPTER 3

REASONS TO GO
TO LAW SCHOOL

I am not going to begin the substance of my book by providing a blasé paragraph about the honor of the legal profession, the gratification of seeking justice on behalf of a client, the confidence that comes with being an expert on something that is complicated and intimidating to many others, and the potential prestige and financial reward of a career in law. You know all of this; some part of this appeals to you (or to your parents) or you would not be reading this book. After all, as one of our survey respondents wrote when asked whether she would recommend others to attend law school, "it's the only way to become a lawyer." If that's your end goal, law school is for you. The real question is, ***do you want to be a lawyer?***

One way to figure that out is to talk to lawyers as I did. The good news is that for all of the negatives you'll read about job prospects, debt, and where the legal field is headed, this is really the part of the book that shows you're not totally off base for wanting to go to law school.

Overall, lawyers feel really good about their own careers and lives. Many of the negative feelings lawyers express have to do with the job market in general, even though only 3 percent of our survey respondents identified themselves as being unemployed. Largely, lawyers claim to be doing the exact things that people go to law school to do.

> When we asked lawyers for the good things about their current jobs, here is what they had to say:
> - 74%—they interact with interesting people (co-workers and clients).
> - 67%—they feel "intellectual stimulation" is a positive aspect of their work.
> - 58%—they feel "personal satisfaction" about their work.
> - Overall, attorneys feel that other good things about their profession are the schedule/hours (53 percent), helping others (50 percent), and financial reward (50 percent).

One survey claimed that as many as 70 percent of lawyers said they would not choose a legal career again.[24] Certainly, some of our respondents fell into this camp. As one litigator with 20 years of experience since graduating from Vermont stated, "Attorneys, by and large, are unhappy. The stress is crushing at times. The raging egos that come along with many lawyers are ludicrous. I would not encourage anyone, except those ready and prepared to tackle the most competitive, dog-eat-dog, status-climbing culture that exists, to attend."

However, the crazy thing—the thing I'm scared to tell you for fear you'll claim I made it up or manipulated it—is that we gave lawyers a series of 10 statements to check only if they applied and the most universal response—76 percent of lawyers

---

[24] Levit and Linder, The Happy Lawyer, Foreword, x.

agreed—was "*I am glad I attended law school.*" **76 percent!** In addition, 67 percent said, "*I am proud to be a lawyer.*" Erin Pace, who has her own family law firm, is one of them:

> I call myself the "neighborhood" lawyer because I assist my community with a lot of everyday-type legal struggles. For example, after completing a divorce for one client, I prepared a lease for her new tenant, amended her living trust, defended her daughter in a debt collection action, and later assisted her in obtaining an insurance settlement after a car accident. The best part about my job is that I get to assist my clients in achieving real and practical results and, at the same time, earn a great living, dictate my own hours, and maintain an office that comports with my integrity and style (i.e., a comfortable, accessible, and professional office)! I sure hated every darn moment of law school, but somehow knew in my heart that it was the absolute right path for me—and I certainly do not regret it for a moment!

Most lawyers feel the same. Only 19 percent feel unappreciated, and only 10 percent say they serve clients whose values conflict with their own. Sixteen percent claim to be "pushing paper" in their current position, 28 percent claim to be overworked, and only 32 percent claim to be underpaid. There were 37 percent who claimed to have job security even though only 16 percent of lawyers overall think that job security is a reason to become a lawyer.

When asked to pick only three downsides of their current job, the #1 response was stress-level (46 percent), followed by pay (36 percent, matching pretty evenly with the 32 percent who claim to be underpaid), and hours (33 percent) (also matching pretty well with the other 53 percent who claim that their schedule/hours is one of the good things about their current jobs). These were the three biggest downsides by a landslide. Other contenders were too much work (22 percent), not enough help (22 percent), and competition in the field (18 percent).

Other responses in the open-ended section included:

- "Lack of respect" (written by someone who went to a Top 10 law school and who has worked for a big firm since graduating 6 to 10 years ago).
- "Generally unsatisfied personally."
- "Meaningless work that does not utilize legal education" (this person is within five years of law school graduation and also commented that he does not interact with clients or make court appearances, which he would like to do).

If you're not sure, then you need to do your research. What do lawyers really do? How much do they make? How do they feel about their professions and lives? Does a law degree really open doors to other careers? Do attorneys feel it was worth the investment of time and money? Consider this book a major part of that research.

Recently, there has been a lot of chatter about whether attending law school pays off (literally).[25] As one law school dean acknowledges, the business consideration of profit has entered the lexicon of academic pursuits.[26] However, it is important to

---

[25] In *Should I Go To Law School? The $100,000 Gamble* (New York: R + S Media, 2011), author Derek Roberti spends a great deal of time analyzing the financial side of the decision. This book also includes a discussion of the personal attributes demonstrating a more likely affinity for the practice of law.

[26] www.nationaljurist.com/content/critical-issues/law-school-worth-it-dean-looks-behind-numbers.

keep in mind that "Choosing to become a lawyer—or anything else—involves more than calculating whether an initial job will yield a reasonable return on the educational investment for the degree it requires."[27] In addition, it's worth noting that this debate is not limited to law: for-profit colleges,[28] four-year colleges,[29] and MBA programs have borne the brunt of the same criticism.[30] However, when it comes right down to it, few people make a fabulous living with only a high school diploma. If you're looking for a sure financial bet, people always need plumbers. That's an example of a solid profession with respectable income that requires business savvy and problem-solving ability. If these are some of the qualities that lead you to law, consider this: just because you are good at business and at solving problems doesn't mean you must be a lawyer. Being a lawyer is one option, perhaps, but it's not the only one. You might think, "But my parents don't want to tell their friends and business associates that their daughter is a plumber." If this is the first thought that comes to your mind, there is a strong likelihood that you are going to law school for the wrong reasons.

In addition to asking whether you are attorney material, ask whether you even want to be an attorney. It is important to talk about the qualities that lawyers must exhibit and the

---

[27] Steven J. Harper, "Great Expectations Meet Painful Realities," *The Circuit Rider: The Journal of the Seventh Circuit Bar Association* (April 2011); www.7thcircuitbar.org/associations/1507/files/Circuit%20Rider%20Vol%2010.pdf.

[28] www.npr.org/2011/05/12/136238528/for-profit-colleges-targeting-people-who-cant-pay.

[29] www.usnews.com/education/blogs/college-cash-101/2008/11/17/is-a-college-degree-really-worth-the-cost.

[30] http://articles.chicagotribune.com/2010-08-10/features/sc-fam-0810-education-college-worth-20100810_1_student-debt-private-colleges-world-of-college-admissions.

skills they must possess to decide whether attending law school and becoming an attorney is a good fit for you. According to the Law School Survey for Student Engagement, more than half of all 1Ls stated their reasons for going to law school were "related to securing a challenging and rewarding career, furthering academic development, achieving financial security, or achieving prestige."[31] In our survey, we asked potential law students what their reasons were for wanting to go to law school and asked lawyers what they felt were good reasons for going to law school. See Table 3.1 for what they had to say.

Table 3.1 Reasons for Going to Law School

Reasons	Lawyer	Law Applicant
Wanting to make a difference in the world.	53 %	55%
Wanting to help people.	63%	65%
Helping companies grow.	30%	25%
Learning to think like a lawyer.	73%	52%
Making a lot of money.	20.2%	43%
Desiring job security.	16%	46%
Not knowing what else to do.	7.9%	9%
Being a good public speaker.	25%	35%
Being a good negotiator.	44%	32%
Enjoying solving problems.	70%	72%

---

[31] http://lssse.iub.edu/pdf/2010/2010_LSSSE_Annual_Survey_Results.pdf.

Wanting a prestigious career.	28%	56%
Serving the local community.	49%	43%
Enjoying researching and writing.	67%	51%
Enjoying arguing.	36%	29%
Desire to enter politics.	36%	22%
Being able to run a business while knowing legal implications.	48%	30%

Let's discuss each of these more in depth.

Learning to Think Like a Lawyer

Law school ruined *The Sixth Sense* for me. Ok, not quite, but almost. Law school changed me. Before going to law school I never knew what would happen at the end of a mystery. During winter break after my first semester, I had to stop reading mysteries because I knew within the first chapter who had "done it." Law school wakes you up. It helps you notice little—relevant—details that you previously would have over-looked. Every time you walk past a *piso mojado* (wet floor) sign in a grocery store, you will think about that slip and fall case from your torts class. Even though I don't practice law today, I know that my brain works better because I think like a lawyer. Every time I sign a permission slip for my children or evaluate someone's personal statement or addendum, I'm thinking about which words and statements are relevant, which are redundant, and which are risky. I help them create an argument.

"Fully 70 percent of lawyers report that the intellectual challenge of law practice 'very well' matched their expectations."[32]

---

[32] Nancy Levit and Douglas O. Linder, *The Happy Lawyer: Making a Good Life in the*

Lawyers listed "learning to think like a lawyer" as being the best reason to go to law school. (In contrast, pre-laws ranked it in the middle of their reasons for going to law school.) Investigative counselor Charles-Eric Gordon says, "Learning 'to think like a lawyer' is well worth law school tuition whether or not one wants to engage in actually practicing law. We live in a complex society and knowing the rules evens the playing field." Chad Lang, a partner in a law firm in Miami, Florida, says, "I think knowledge of the law is empowering regardless of your intended occupation. And if you are going to practice law for a living, and you find the right practice area and people to work with, the experience can be incredibly rewarding."

> My father was not an attorney, but as an urban planner, worked with land use attorneys and was very involved in the bar. My mentors from high school and college had connections to the law; they were not practicing attorneys but impressed upon me how valuable a legal education is and I grew up knowing I wanted a legal education.
>
> It is absolutely one of the best "thinking" degrees. Law school teaches you such a valuable thought process, and the importance of analytical and logical reasoning. As a business owner, I can process complicated business challenges with an analytical focus because of my law degree, and it gives me credibility with clients as well. I would really recommend law school even for those not looking to practice law but as a thinking degree.
>
> I went to law school consciously knowing I was not planning on practicing, but went just for the degree. I

Law (New York: Oxford University Press, 2010), 52.

wanted to study at a graduate level and the law school curriculum was the most appealing. As a Marine, I had the GI bill, which made it cost effective, and I knew that I did not have to take on student loans.

In between, recruiters came to campus, the money offered was excellent, and I took a legal position at a big firm, but that job didn't play to my strengths. A lot of time was spent isolated, researching, and I am a people person who liked client contact. I wrote a book after seeing people in the law firm world who had excellent legal skills but didn't have leadership skills and saw a niche/opportunity based on what I had learned as a Marine to teach those in the legal profession leadership skills since leadership is so important in the legal field and for entrepreneurs. I wanted to help people understand leadership in a practical way and decided to start my own firm—a consulting firm not a law firm. My advice for those applying to law school is to know why you are going to law school. If it is just to get a high-paying job, really reconsider and look at lots of different paths to a high-paying career because a legal profession is not a sure thing to a high-paying job. It's a sure thing for a great education, but an expensive education that can leave you with no financial freedom to go do what you really wanted. Know seriously what careers beyond law school look like, and make sure you are willing to make the financial commitment.

—Courtney Lynch earned her law degree at William and Mary before creating Lead Star. Lead Star's clients include ESPN, Cisco Systems, Best Buy, Executive Women International, the

Junior League, the U.S. Senate, Department of Health and Human Services, and the University of Michigan. She is the best-selling author of *Leading from the Front*. She was awarded the National Stevie Award for Best Female Entrepreneur and *BusinessWeek* profiled her achievements as a leadership expert.

Having the ability to think like a lawyer is really what makes the degree so versatile. Here are some lawyers' comments on this subject:

- John Thyne III, a graduate of the University of Tulsa, currently resides in California and holds three law-related positions at once: he is a solo practitioner in workers compensation law, the CEO of a successful and groundbreaking real estate company, and also a professor at our local law school. According to him, "Having a law degree, whether you practice law or not, is an excellent way to help others and yourself by understanding the law and learning to use it as a tool for success."

- James Rudolph graduated from Boston College more than 20 years ago and is the managing partner of his own law firm. "Even if you do not intend to practice law, [law school] provides an excellent background. One of my sons graduated law school two years ago, but does not practice; he is in the real estate business. My other son is in his second year of law school and intends to practice law, at least for a while."

- "Law plays a role in so many areas of our lives," offered Sonia Pressman Fuentes (who graduated from law school more than 20 years ago). "The knowledge one gains in law school stands one in good stead for the rest of one's life whatever one does." This theme was present in many of our survey's responses. "In the game of life, lawyers are the people who know the rules, make the rules, understand the rules, and know how to change the rules. You can use a law degree to become whoever you want to be and do whatever you love doing most," according to Laurie Gray, owner of Socratic Parenting LLC and a graduate of Indiana University-Bloomington.

- Kevin Houchin, author of *Fuel the Spark: 5 Guiding Values for Success in Law School and Beyond* (New York: Morgan James Publishing, 2009), began his own law firm and mediation practice after graduating from the University of Iowa in his thirties. He adds, "A JD is the quickest, easiest, and least expensive doctoral degree out there and opens more doors than any other academic experience."

"Varied" appears to be the word of choice for many attorneys who feel they benefitted from a legal education, no matter their current positions or the schools they attended. Marlynn Jones, a friend of mine from law school, is now the Assistant Director of Athletics for Compliance at North Carolina Central University. She says, "A law degree enables one to be very *versatile* and provides the opportunity to be able to *do so many different things* in so many different careers." My friend Anita Presser, a graduate of Yale who now stays home with her children and runs an investment business, agrees. "The law allows for *varied and flexible career choices*." Lastly, Julie Saltoun, a graduate of Loyola who previously served as executive director of a nonprofit and is now of-counsel at a firm doing contract work, adds "law school is a good jumping off point for many *varied careers* and provides a solid useful education for many careers."

> In my case, with my law degree, I was able to be an investment banker, in-house counsel, op-ed columnist, and author. No other degree except for the JD offers so many possibilities. More than knowing the law, the JD degree gives you a more invaluable skill set—the ability to think in a structured way to get to a solution. This type of skill set can be leveraged in almost any field. The only limit is your imagination.
> —Jasper Kim, Associate Professor/Department Chair, Ewha Womans University, Korea

Jessica Silverstein, owner of Attorney's Counsel (a resume review service for attorneys) and a graduate of Brooklyn Law School, states that

Law school, regardless of cost, is an excellent education and credential to have achieved. You are able to see the world in a different way and connect with people who intimately understand what you do and the hard work you did to achieve your degree. I will always be proud to be a lawyer. While there are many factors involved in any decision, I truly believe that law school graduates who are dissatisfied with their careers have not explored every available option.

I will always think a law degree is a valuable degree to do whatever you want with. People say, "Oh, people hate lawyers." Everyone knows how hard you have to work and how smart you have to be, and respect is due to the degree. It's not a way to make a million dollars a year, but I would never discourage someone from going who wanted to go. Law school was wonderful— I loved the classes, I loved thinking in that way; it made global history make more sense, and all these different parts of life made more sense.

One attorney, who has worked in international human rights law in Santiago, Chile since graduating from the University of Arizona, would encourage people to go to law school "if people are strategic about going to law school (selecting the school, the financing of it, post-graduation plans), it is an experience that can benefit everyone. Law school changes you as a person, I think in a good way, regardless of whether you end up 'practicing' law."

One graduate of the University of Michigan who now works in business says, "Law school can teach you valuable life skills that will last a lifetime."

Enjoying Solving Problems

This reason for going to law school seems to be perfectly in line with reality because it's reason #1 for pre-laws and listed as #2 for law grads. A law professor who responded to our survey said that attending law school "is a terrific way to learn how to help solve society's problems." Lawyers are problem solvers. Whether figuring out how to protect assets for a company or an elderly couple, or how to draft a contract to foresee events that could possibly take place or deciding how much a case is worth during settlement negotiations, finding solutions— often, creative solutions—is the core of a lawyer's job. However, I find that some law school applicants have idealistic views of how much influence a single lawyer can have on creating over-arching policy or changing the laws themselves.

I confess that I was one of those law school applicants who hoped to eradicate employment discrimination, and it took several labor and employment law classes and working on the defense side to see that the real work is in educating companies and crafting their sexual harassment policies. It's not big and it's not sexy, but that's the kind of change a lawyer can make *if* a client is willing to pay for it. Of course, if you work for the Department of Justice or the Equal Employment Opportunity Commission, you can do more, but you're still not writing the laws and you're limited regarding what cases you can pursue. You are, however, part of enforcing the law and that is a pretty cool thing.

Wanting to Help People and Serving the Local Community

Wanting to help people was #2 for prospective lawyers and #4 for lawyers. Serving the local community was second to last for prospective lawyers and right in the middle for graduates. Allan Ghitterman, an attorney with 55 years of experience since graduating from UCLA, is an example of how a law degree allows you to serve others. "The law is a valuable aspect of a civilized community and contributes to the quality of life in any community. Lawyers help people, and that is an important element of community spirit." His work serves as a great example of how lawyers impact their communities: he has been an active board member and supporter of local organizations including Legal Aid and Human Rights Watch and, in his retirement, serves as a volunteer judge.

Wanting to Make a Difference in the World

I expected this to rank in the top three reasons to go to law school for pre-laws and in the bottom three for practicing lawyers, but law school applicants proved to be more pragmatic than I expected, and lawyers were less jaded than I imagined. (Perhaps these prospective applicants had learned from my first book where I warned people against writing in their personal statements that they "wanted to make a difference.")

"It's a great career where you can definitely make a difference if it fits your aptitude," stated Samuel Coffey, a partner at the personal injury firm of Abramowitz, Pomerantz & Coffey in Fort Lauderdale, Florida. Kay Barnes Baxter, a partner at Swetman Baxter Massenburg LLC in New Orleans, Louisiana, says, "I find it to be a fulfilling career where I can make a difference, use my mind, and continually learn new things and meet interesting people."

One lawyer who graduated more than 21 years ago from the University of Toronto says, "The two areas in which I have found some satisfaction are criminal defense (where you really can turn around a young person's life, sometimes) and military law—where your clients are doing things that really can change the world."

Enjoying Research and Writing

Lawyers ranked this as the third best reason to go to law school (even if prospective lawyers were a bit less enthused). What lawyers know and prospective lawyers have yet to learn is that legal arguments are really made in writing and oral arguments are usually only to supplement or further explain the written motions or trial briefs. Legal arguments are formed by researching relevant cases to serve as precedent and presenting the facts of your case in such a way as to persuade the judge that the precedent you cite is applicable to your case. "If [you] are good at and enjoy writing and logic and are very organized/detail-oriented, these are a plus. If [you] lack any of these, [you] will hate being a lawyer," says a graduate of Columbia who is now senior counsel for a corporation.

Entry into Politics

A former law school classmate of mine who holds political office said, "A law degree is like a road. Entering politics was a destination. You don't have to be a lawyer to reach that destination, and I probably would have wound up in politics without a law degree. That being said, many of my donors and supporters originate from contacts I've made through the legal community." Jeff Hauser, a graduate of NYU and a political consultant, decided not to practice public interest law because he learned that politicians are really the ones who can change the law.

Making a Lot of Money

We talk a lot about money in this book—what lawyers make, which areas of law pay the most, and what you can expect to make right out of law school. Obviously, becoming a lawyer is *one* way to make a good living. Of course, it's not the only way. Many entrepreneurs, doctors, and law enforcement officers with overtime make above six figures. But, yes, law can be very lucrative. For 43 percent of pre-laws, making a lot of money was among their reasons for applying to law school, but only 20 percent of lawyers said this was a good reason to go to law school. Part of this may be because it takes years before most lawyers make a lot of money. You need to be prepared to weather a few years making less than what you may be making in your current job as a sales associate or paralegal. However, if you can manage your lifestyle and debt load, chances are that between 5 and 10 years out of law school you'll be making significantly more than your current salary. We go into compensation in more depth in Chapter 5.

Job Security

For 46 percent of law school applicants, this was a reason for applying to law school, but only 16 percent of practicing lawyers agreed! One recent graduate of Boston College was laid off from his job with Milbank Tweed and, since 2009, has been working in the government relations department of another large firm. He says, "Law is no longer a stable profession. I would only recommend that an individual attend law school if he or she is passionate about becoming a lawyer and would get into a top-rated school."

Whenever someone else is responsible for hiring and firing, it leaves you without control. Even if you're a rainmaker (bringing in a lot of money for the firm), someone else may decide they want the business you're bringing in and fire you. You will be susceptible to changes in the marketplace. However, one thing that a law degree does give you is the opportunity to work for yourself. You can always "hang a shingle" and be the one who decides how much you work and what you get paid (as long as you're bringing the money in, the division of it is up to you when you're self employed). You'll learn more about being your own boss in Chapter 11.

Wanting a Prestigious Career

For 54 percent of pre-laws, this was among their reasons for applying to law school, but only 28 percent of lawyers felt this was a good reason. I think this goes back to the parent issue—who are you trying to impress and why? It might be better to spend your money on a good therapist than an LSAT prep course (unless you find solving logic games therapeutic, and then that's a pretty good sign that you'd enjoy a law career).

Not Knowing What Else to Do

You have a general impression of what it's like to be a lawyer, and—as someone who is an excellent writer, speaks well, and is bright—believe you have the qualities to make a go of it. However, you may be one of the many law school applicants and potential applicants who are wavering on your decision to attend law school.

Only 43 percent of people planning to apply to law school in the next year (for the fall 2012 cycle) say they will "absolutely attend" law school. Of those who are slated to start law school in the next few months, only 57 percent say they will absolutely attend. This is, of course, why my friends who are deans of admission at law schools ranked outside of the top 14 are chasing people down on their waitlists with phone calls and scholarship offers. It's important, however, to look at the reasons why people are unsure that they will follow through with their law school plans.

You can blame the job market for your wavering if it offers you a logical reason not to move forward with your career; however, it's not entirely a bad thing to take this extra time for introspection to make sure your expectations are in line with reality. After all, law school will still be there in a year. Some of the older applicants I work with feel very rushed—they want to start immediately so they can get to where they are going; but, for the rest of you, it really won't hurt to take a year and contemplate.

Figure 3.1 **If you are not certain about whether you will apply to law school, what factors are the reason for your uncertainty? Please check all that apply.**

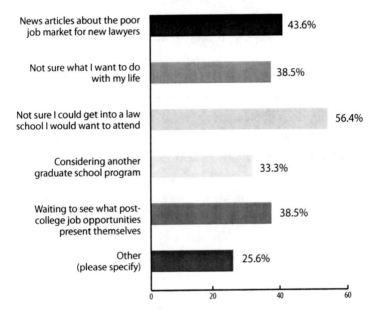

In ranking order, here are the reasons law school applicants and prospective applicants cite for their uncertainty (see Figure 3.1):

#1 Not being sure they could get into a law school they would want to attend.

#2 News articles about the poor job market for new lawyers.

#3 A three-way tie between three responses: not sure
     what I want to do with my life, waiting to see what
     post-college job opportunities present themselves, and
     considering another graduate school program.

People also listed financial reasons (not sure if they could
afford it or qualify for loans) and taking time off to work in a
law firm before starting.

Fewer than 10 percent of both lawyers and prospective law
school applicants felt going to law school was a good idea if you
didn't know what else to do.[33] This number probably would
have been higher a few years ago, but has diminished in recent
years given the extent of press about the legal job market. It may
also be low because prospective lawyers are embarrassed to admit
that they don't know what else to do. For many, law school was
the default option. "'Drift' or 'default' decisions occur because
it is so overwhelming to make a choice. People [applying to
law school today] were raised in a kid-centric programmed time
where they always knew their next steps. There is something
familiar and comforting in deciding to go to law school rather
than trying to make your own way." According to Shannon
Kelley, co-author of *Undecided: How to Ditch the Endless Quest
for Perfect and Find the Career—and Life—That's Right for
You* (Berkeley, CA: Seal Press, 2011), "Having scholarships or
parents paying for law school encourages a 'drift' decision," says
Kelley. She says people fall easily into thinking, "I know how to
do school, school is familiar."[34]

This was certainly true for Martha Kimes, author of *Ivy*

---

[33] Professor Thane Rosenbaum thinks students who are unsure of their choice
to attend law school are the most defensive about their career choices (interview,
06/30/2011).

[34] Interview, 05/24/2011.

Briefs and a graduate of Columbia. In her book, she wrote "I must admit that my decision to go to law school was made by default more than it was fueled by a raging desire to practice law. I wanted so badly to be an adult, to be taken seriously, but I had no idea how to go about it."[35] In a telephone interview, she elaborated on this (with the benefit that 20 years' hindsight often offers): "I finished college and didn't know what to do, and the pre-law counselor says, 'you can do anything with a law degree.' I knew a lot of people who were in law school because their dad was a lawyer, but I didn't know that many people who knew why they wanted to be there. As I connect with them on Facebook and LinkedIn, I see that of my former classmates, maybe half of them are still lawyers."[36]

Gretchen Rubin is a graduate of Yale, where she served as editor of the *Yale Law Journal* before clerking for Supreme Court Justice Sandra Day O'Connor. After practicing law in New York, Gretchen decided to become a full-time author. Her recent book, *The Happiness Project* (New York: Harper, 2009), is the #1 selling book in the "Happiness" category on Amazon. com. Although she was obviously a very capable law student (who even published a note in the *Yale Law Journal* as a 1L), she says she only went to law school because she didn't know what else to do.

> If you were good at reading, writing, and research, you went to law school because everyone said "you'll be new and improved and it doesn't really limit your choices, and it makes you better prepared for anything you would want to do." She says in some ways going

---

[35] Martha Kimes, *Ivy Briefs: True Tales of a Neurotic Law Student* (New York: Atria Books/Simon & Schuster, 2007), 7.

[36] Interview, 05/24/2011.

to law school is an easy career decision to make. "Law is a prescribed path—you don't have to figure out, for example, how to get a job in network news. There is a way to do it: take the LSAT, apply to law school, etc. It seemed like it would only help you later, and it's very clear what is expected of you. That's a very alluring proposition for people who don't have a strong sense of what it is they want to do. I wonder if a lot of it is people pretending they know what they want but they really don't. They know they need a reason to go, so they manufacture something. It's hard to figure out what to do with yourself. No one wants to do the exercises in *What Color Is Your Parachute* and look deep within their soul.[37]

For years, whenever people have told me they only want to go to law school if they can go to Harvard, Yale, or Stanford, I have told them that they don't really want to go to law school. Gretchen agrees.

It's a big warning sign—if you want something, you will start at the bottom. If you only want to go to Harvard, Yale, or Stanford, you don't really want to go. If you're only going to do it for a fancy pants credential, you don't want a law degree—you want the fancy pants credential.

Say to yourself, how happy does it make my parents. If it makes your parents really, really, really happy that's a sign that you need to make sure that YOU really want to go. The approval of the people we love is sweet, but it's not enough to build a foundation of a happy life. Even if your parents are paying for you to go to law school

---

doesn't mean it's the right thing for you. Sometimes if everyone wants you to go to law school you think it's got to be a good idea, but in the end—it's you. The whole process is so grueling. It doesn't feel like you make a decision out of inertia or indecision, but people are not acting with self knowledge. The further you get down that road, it gets harder to turn.[38]

As a clerk, Gretchen saw people at the Supreme Court who loved the law, talked about the law during lunch, read law journals in their free time, and she realized that although "law was one of the ruling passions of their life" it was not one of hers. "Law is a great profession for some people: my father is a very happy lawyer. Too many people go to it, but for some people it's not a good choice." Gretchen has seen an undercurrent reason for going to law school that she deems "dangerous," namely going into entertainment law because you really want to be a screenwriter but you are scared of failure and want something to fall back on. "But it's not the same thing at all," she says. "Being a lawyer in that area is *not* the same thing as doing it. Being an entertainment lawyer is being a contract lawyer—it's not like writing a screenplay."[39]

Martha Kimes, in *Ivy Briefs*, says readers often reach out to her to ask whether they should go to law school. In response, she says,

> Go *if* you want to go, *if* you know why you want to go, *if* you have a realistic idea of what you're going to get out of it. It's not a good way to approach it to say, 'It'll work out in the end.' I knew a lot of people who

<hr />

[38] Interview, 06/21/2011.

[39] For more on what entertainment law attorneys really do, see Chapter 13.

were in law school because they were told they could do anything with a law degree, but if you really want to go into politics or open a cupcake shop, then going to law school may not be the best thing.[40]

> Don't become a lawyer because you like to argue. Those students make the worst lawyers. Go to law school because you want to help people and do it within the parameters of the legal system. Do it because you are good at spotting issues, seeing both sides of a problem, and finding resolution. Do it because you enjoy reading and writing.
> —Kira Willig, a family law attorney, mediator, and adjunct professor

Ask yourself honestly why you want to go to law school based on your idea of a good career for yourself. "Maybe you'll see you don't need a law degree to do what you want or maybe you'll find that you do need it and that's great." She also warns people whose purpose in going to law school is to work for the American Civil Liberties Union or for human rights groups or as a public defender or prosecutor to look into who gets these jobs and how hard they are to obtain. "A lot of these jobs are super competitive and you don't even know if you would be able to live in the place you want and have the job you want."

For the person who passes all the tests and still wants to go to law school, Gretchen offers hope and encouragement. "It's an amazing education. I'm such a better writer and [I] understand the world better. It is extremely valuable, but it comes with an opportunity cost. Is it the right trade-off for you?"

---

[40] Interview, 05/24/2011.

Thane Rosenbaum in The Myth of Moral Justice, *states,*

> Most students attend law school for the wrong reason.
> I see this all the time. In a culture that defines people
> by what they do, being a lawyer produces a satisfyingly
> external self-definition, even though, internally, most
> law students would be much better off doing something
> else. Somehow, over the past 25 years, law and busi-
> ness degrees have achieved unparalleled, and perhaps
> undeserved, cachet. There was a time when teaching
> primary and high schools offered both job security
> and great spiritual reward. Today, few college students
> believe such jobs are dignified or lucrative enough even
> to be called professions, though many of those students
> would make terrific teachers . . . . So these misguided
> seekers of American happiness apply to law schools,
> not sure why they even would want to be lawyers, not
> sure what a lawyer even does. Many have told me that
> a decision not to attend law school would disappoint
> parents, spouses, neighbors, and friends, those who are
> impressed with the law degree but privileged not to
> have to do any of this kind of work.[41]

Gretchen Rubin gave this advice:

> If you have no good reason to go to law school, don't
> go to law school. People say it opens doors, but it is not
> true. This does not keep your options open: they are
> more open before you go. [Law school is] very expen-
> sive and very time consuming. [Ask yourself] "what
> else could I be doing for three years?" A lot of people

---

[41] Thane Rosenbaum, *The Myth of Moral Justice: Why Our Legal System Fails to Do What's Right* (New York: HarperCollins, 2004), 289.

don't particularly want to go, then have crushing debt but they have to work as lawyers because it's the only thing that will pay them enough to pay down their debt, and they could've done whatever they wanted [if they hadn't gone to law school].

CHAPTER 4

TV VERSUS REALITY

EVERY generation has its legal dramas. Some are high glamour (*LA Law*); some are gritty (*Law and Order*); some show sophisticated, cold, wealthy lawyers (*The Firm*); some feature street-smart lawyers (*The Lincoln Lawyer, The Rainmaker*); and some show lawyers fighting for justice (*Erin Brockovich, A Civil Action*). In almost every law-based show or movie, the lawyer hero ends up making a difference for someone else, and/or being redeemed somehow from a life that is materialistic or self-centered. Sometimes they do it almost by mistake (*My Cousin Vinny*). Whatever the story, it's exciting: who wouldn't aspire to a life of making an argument in court, then five minutes later taking a big check from another client in a fancy conference room with floor-to-ceiling windows on the 47th floor, then having "relations" with a secretary, then taking a client out to a four-star dinner (before scheduling a weekend custody visit with your kids)?

The *Wall Street Journal* recently printed, "The Case of the Loopy Lawyers; Frat-Party Antics and Self-Doubt Are the Stuff of Today's Legal Dramas: Where's Atticus Finch?" The remarkable thing is that this wasn't another of the *Journal's* commentaries on the legal profession and trends in the legal marketplace—it was in the Review section of the weekend edition, talking about the new TV show *Franklin and Bash*.[42] This great quote came from that article:

> The entire legal profession has come under scrutiny, and lawyers fear the future, as job losses mount and the "billable hour" gives way to less lucrative arrangements. Attorneys are now being depicted not just as unethical charmers but as conflicted souls who are unsure about whether they entered the right profession. Some act as if they hope to be thrown out; others simply walk away.

This hit the nail on the head—not just describing the new TV show (which I don't have time to see because I'm busy watching *The Bachelorette* during my one designated TV night), but of the current feeling young lawyers have about the profession at this moment in time. I think it would have been different two years ago, and I don't think the change is permanent; however, it's definitely capturing current sentiment. It should be noted that the article was written by a law professor at Fordham University who directs the Forum on Law, Culture & Society. [43]

So who are these people who become lawyers, and what do they do if not daydream about dancing babies (like *Ally McBeal*) or sleep with their assistant district attorneys (as alluded to on *Law & Order*) or work from the back of their cars and have two ex-wives (as in *The Lincoln Lawyer*)? Are these fictional charac-

---

[42] Thane Rosenbaum, "The Case of the Loopy Lawyers; Frat-Party Antics and Self-Doubt Are the Stuff of Today's Legal Dramas: Where's Atticus Finch?" *Wall Street Journal* (June 18, 2011), C3.

[43] I was so fascinated by this piece that I looked up Professor Rosenbaum, noticed that he was also a University of Miami graduate, and contacted him. This is another great example of what happens when you reach outside your comfort zone to connect with people. As a result, I was able to include more insights from Professor Rosenbaum in Chapter 3 and Chapter 10.

ters at all in line with reality? In my experience, they are not. My friends who are practicing law—whether they are serving as prosecutors, in-house counsel, personal injury lawyers, family law attorneys, or city attorneys—are pretty normal people living normal lives. They work 9 to 10 hours a day, see their children at night, and enjoy weekends with their families (even if they have to work for a few hours on a Sunday afternoon). They play golf or tennis, enjoy nice (but not crazily luxurious) vacations, and they treat their staff, colleagues, court personnel, and other lawyers civilly. They are universally bright, savvy, good with people, and responsible; involved in community activities; and try to lead good lives. It's not television worthy (even reality television), but it's a nice life.

It's easy to consider the grand versions of law and see yourself in that role: standing in front of a judge arguing zealously on behalf of a client, playing Maggie McFierce to Matthew McConaughey's *Lincoln Lawyer*. But day in and day out, are you a good fit for getting every paper submitted to the judge or opposing counsel on time, for returning client phone calls quickly, for spending hours on a beautiful Sunday afternoon writing motions? How do you feel about spending your lunch hour with prospective clients and referral sources? Do you absolutely hate triple-checking your writing before it's submitted, looking up rules, and intruding into people's personal lives?

Think about what you do well. For example, I'm too squeamish to be a doctor, too structured to be an actor, and not disciplined enough to be a teacher. I love to work out and do so regularly and brutally, but I'd be a terrible personal trainer because I can't keep count while carrying on a conversation. If I'd entered any of those careers, even if I were smart enough and talented enough to be successful, I would not have been happy. Many people who entered the law and now regret it are people who did not think critically about what they bring to the table and whether their personalities make them a good fit for a life in law. You will hear from quite a few of them throughout this book, but let's start by analyzing what qualities and skills lawyers use in their jobs on a daily basis.

Figure 4.1 **What are the most important traits for success in your field? Please check all that apply.**

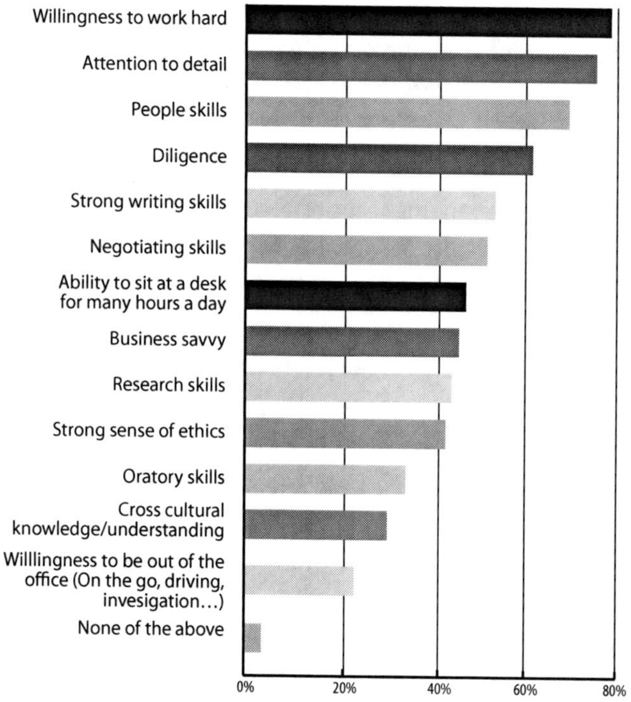

Although TV lawyers may rely on their looks and on esoteric loopholes, real lawyers say these are the things they do every day:

- Utilizing people skills—78%
- Using writing skills—77%
- Solving problems—72%
- Helping people/businesses—64%
- Using public speaking skills—62%
- Using negotiation skills—62%
- Using business skills—57%
- Being an advocate—53%
- Making a difference—51%
- Being a manager—40%
- Making the world a better place—32%
- Being a policy maker—20%
- Making the world a more fair place—33%

Of the 13 traits (see Figure 4.1) we asked about, there were five clear winners—these traits were universally acknowledged as being crucial:

#1—Willingness to work hard (80%)

#2—Attention to detail (77%)

#3—People skills (72%)

#4—Diligence (69%)

#5—Strong writing skills (63%)

One response was nearly unanimous: a "willingness to work hard." Close behind that were "attention to detail," "people skills," "diligence," and "strong writing skills." If these five descriptions don't fit with your skill set, you are likely to be miserable as an attorney. Here are some of the comments from lawyers about the traits required for success in their fields:

- Bret A. Stone, an attorney who says he loves what he does and is passionate about his field of law, says: "I once heard a quote about being a lawyer: 'It's a way to make a good living, but it's not a good way to make a living.' Lawyers work hard. There is definitely stress."

- A San Francisco attorney says the most important aspects to success in BigLaw are "Patience, thick skin, self-awareness, quiet confidence, flexibility, asking questions, taking the time to think before reacting, appearing to be calm/in control even if you're about to soil yourself, building professional relationships, and truly respecting your colleagues at all levels—clients, partners, associates, staff, legal secretaries. Trust me, you can't get anything done as an attorney without the secretaries, file clerks, and courtroom staff on your side. The more they are willing to go to bat for you, the better you look when you are able to solve problems that other lawyers are freaking out about. People skills are essential."

- Rob Egenolf, who has been practicing law for more than 25 years, says the most important traits for any attorney are, "Intelligence, a sense of humor, the ability to read quickly and retain information well, humility, a thick skin, the ability to multitask."

- An attorney who works for a federal agency believes that strong writing skills are essential in almost every legal field. "I spend most of the day massaging sentences and making sure policy decisions are intertwined with sound legal arguments. I also read a lot. I think in order to be a good writer, one must be well read and not just legally. I think creative reading can also make you a better writer and, in turn, a better lawyer."

Attention to detail can be learned, as can writing skills if you begin with some basic competency and work hard at it. In fact, attention to detail is what makes a strong writer. However, people skills, diligence, and a willingness to work hard are things that you either have or you don't. You can build on the beginnings of these by reaching outside of your comfort zone. For example, I was never comfortable at parties until I ran for president of the Student Bar Association at my law school. I knew I had to go out and talk to people on Thursday nights in Coconut Grove, the traditional happy hour time and place for law students at the University of Miami. Although this was not my usual scene, I did it and met new people; some of them are still my Facebook friends today, and a few of them are even quoted throughout this book.

You need motivation and confidence to go out in the world, represent yourself well, and build relationships. What's absolutely crucial is that you are *willing* to do it. If you're not, then you're going to have a hard time even in a government job because unless you meet the higher-ups and represent yourself well, you won't be promoted. Every aspect of being a lawyer requires self-promotion. (For more about this, read what Deborah Epstein Henry has to say in Chapter 9.)

Outside of these five core traits, different jobs within law can require very different skill sets. If you don't do well sitting in one place, then you can choose an area of law that doesn't keep you at a desk all day. BigLaw is out, but being a public defender or workers compensation attorney might be great career choices for you. In Chapter 17, different areas of law are discussed to help you determine what areas of law might be a good fit for you.

Of course, it's not just about whether you have the skills to be a good lawyer or whether you are a good fit for the law. "When you come out of law school, your career decisions are influenced by things outside of your control," says Gretchen

Rubin. You can't control the marketplace or the economy or demand within your niche. Government entities may not be hiring. Nonprofit fundraising numbers might be down. Law firms might be scaling back their entering classes of associates and restructuring how they bill their clients. Divorces and bankruptcies may be increasing while mergers and acquisitions might be disappearing.

> *Deborah Epstein Henry, the author of* Law & Reorder, *is a legal industry consultant who advises clients on workplace restructuring, talent management, work/life balance, and the retention and promotion of lawyers. She told me,*
>
> > *If you are thinking about going to law school, understand the marketplace, not just your individual needs, desires, and strengths. You need to understand the environment within which you would practice. You need to understand how legal employers work, what the market demands, and you need to look at trends in the legal services market.*[44]

The difference between the skills needed for a real-life lawyer and those demonstrated by someone who plays one on TV should be apparent by now. Not one lawyer we surveyed mentioned the necessity of a luxury car, designer suit, or attractive legal assistant to be successful in the daily practice of law. If this is a sincere disappointment to you, you may be better suited to a career in the studios of Hollywood rather than in the Los Angeles County Courthouse, especially after reading the next chapter about how much lawyers really earn.

---

[44] Deborah Epstein Henry, *Law & Reorder: Legal Industry Solutions for Restructure, Retention, Promotion & Work/Life Balance* (Chicago: American Bar Association, 2010).

CHAPTER 5

THE $100,000 QUESTION:

HOW MUCH MONEY DO LAWYERS REALLY MAKE?

O NE of the considerations in deciding whether to attend law school is how you envision your lifestyle, both in terms of how much you work and how much you make. It turns out there is a huge salary range for lawyers depending on their employer, specialty, and location.[45] In recent months, the *Wall Street Journal* published an article highlighting the handful of lawyers in New York City who now bill their time at over $1,000 per hour.[46] At the same time, in Table 5.1, we see Payscale reports showing the median salaries in various legal professions topping out at about $130,000 per year.[47] It's important to know before you start spending money to earn your JD what you are likely to earn during the span of your career.

---

[45] Gender may also be a factor. www.cleveland.com/business/index.ssf/2010/07/women_attorneys_still_falling.html.

[46] http://online.wsj.com/article/SB10001424052748704071304576160362028728234.html.

[47] www.payscale.com/research/US/People_with_Jobs_that_require_a_Law_%2f_Legal_Degree/Salary.

Table 5.1 **Median Salaries According to Payscale**

Job	National Salary Data
Associate Attorney	$69,992
Corporate Counsel	$107,523
General Counsel	$133,569
Entry-Level Attorney	$52,803
Corporate Attorney	$99,927
Assistant General Counsel	$124,743
Staff Attorney	$65,891

Some big law firms (pre-recession) made headlines by paying recent law school graduates $160,000 per year. This is the magic number that continues to reside in the heads of law school applicants. However, this is the exception to the exception, and not the norm, especially in the current employment market. Although one of my former clients, a recent graduate of Stanford, has one of these high-paying jobs and says that most of his classmates who wanted them also have them, one law professor I spoke with (from a non-elite law school) says, "Prospective law students need to think about $60,000-a-year jobs and make decisions based upon that number." "Many law graduates received low starting salaries, a smaller number obtained large starting salaries, and there was not much middle ground."[48] Our survey data (Figure 2.6) relating to whether people make more or less than the median attorney's salary confirm this trend. Of course, people working in the public

---

[48] Levit and Linder, *The Happy Lawyer*, 135.

sector have salaries that grow and then cap after a certain amount of time.

A recent article in *Forbes Magazine* discusses how misleading salary information is for those considering law school:

> *U.S. News* lists the median private sector starting salary out of school at $160,000 with no variation for each of their top 15 schools. No. 16 Vanderbilt finally breaks the streak with starting pay of $147,500 listed on their *U.S. News* page. . . . Schools like NYU, Penn, UCLA, and many others advertise the $160K number on their school websites. Some schools tout $160,000 as the median starting pay for all grads, while others qualify it as salaries in the private sector or for practicing law in private practice. . . . [T]here is a huge disparity in salaries for law school graduates. A small percentage of them will make $160,000 after graduation. Most will not.[49]

The national median salary for the Class of 2009, based on those working full-time and reporting a salary, was $72,000, unchanged from the previous year, and the national mean was $93,454. However, as the *Jobs & JDs* report details, because some large law firm salaries cluster in the $160,000 range while many other salaries cluster in the $40,000 to $65,000 range, relatively few salaries were actually near the median or mean. The national median salary at law firms was $130,000, compared with $125,000 the prior year, and the national mean at law firms was $115,254. Medians for government, judicial clerkships, and public interest jobs changed little from 2008 at $52,000, $50,000, and $42,800 respectively.[50]

---

[49] http://blogs.forbes.com/kurtbadenhausen/2011/03/23/law-school-graduates-do-not-make-160000/.

[50] www.nalp.org/09salpressrel. NALP, The Association for Legal Career Professionals.

Salaries don't grow exponentially within each employment branch as shown by the Bureau of Labor Statistics reports that the median annual wages of all lawyers (no matter how long they've been out of law school) were $110,590 in 2008. The middle chunk of lawyers earn between $74,980 and $163,320.[51] Stock options of a publicly traded entity are not an option in the law firm model, and the shareholder status of a law firm is based only on your individual and total firm earnings, not a buyout or public valuation, so is usually significantly more limited in value in the law firm. Median annual wages in the areas employing the largest number of lawyers are seen in Table 5.2.

Table 5.2 **Median Annual Wages in the Industries Employing the Largest Numbers of Lawyers**

Management of companies and enterprises	$145,770
Federal Executive Branch	126,080
Legal services	116,550
Local government	82,590
State government	78,540

Source: Bureau of Labor Statistics; www.bls.gov/oco/ocos053.htm.

Judges reported median annual wages of $110,220. The middle 50 percent earned between $51,760 and $141,190. The top 10 percent earned more than $162,140.[52]

A recent survey by PayScale reviewed mid-career median total compensation for those in the private sector.[53] This showed one

[51] www.bls.gov/oco/ocos053.htm#outlook.

[52] www.bls.gov/oco/ocos272.htm.

[53] http://blogs.forbes.com/kurtbadenhausen/2011/03/08/the-best-law-schools-for-getting-rich/.

key attraction to the legal profession: after 20 years in the field, people continue to see significant salary growth.[54] However, this means you need to stay in the field to make the real money and not leave to pursue other (personal or professional) endeavors. I have always believed that many people who are practicing law 5 and 10 years after graduation are making significantly more than they made when first employed as a lawyer. Certainly my own experience as a first-year associate whose salary increased from $65,000 to $95,000 in a year's time confirms that, as does the fact that my husband's salary doubled within five years of his law school graduation, followed by another 50 percent jump in the next five years. According to our survey (see Table 5.3), 34 percent of attorneys say they made significantly more money five years after law school graduation and 31 percent said they made significantly more money 10 years after graduation.

Table 5.3 **Expected Earnings 10 Years from Now in Comparison to $105,000**

	Currently Make	Expect to Make in 10 Years[55]
Significantly less:	30%	6.2%
Slightly less:	14%	7.4%
About the same:	7.4%	12.4%
Slightly more:	14.7%	17.4%
Significantly more:	33.7%	49%

[54] According to Al Lee, PayScale's Director of Quantitative Analysis, lawyers have a unique advantage. He says it is one of the few professions where there can be a significant gain in pay after 20 years on the job. That is not typically the case in other careers.

55 7.4% responded "Not applicable because I do not plan to be working in 10 years."

In law, as in most professions, pay increases with years of experience. Data on overall lawyers' salaries compiled by the Labor Department show that the median lawyer makes some $113,000 per year (meaning that 50 percent of lawyers make that much or more). Even lawyers at the 25th percentile of pay in the profession make about $76,000 per year. You have to go to the bottom 10 percent of the profession to find lawyers making under $55,000 per year.[56]

Salary alone is not indicative of more discretionary income, of course. Lawyers in big cities (New York, Boston, San Francisco, etc.) make more money but also face significantly higher costs of living.[57] A great resource for seeing what lawyers make in different geographic areas is www.cbsalary.com/salaries/Lawyer. For example, this website states that the average salary for lawyers nationwide is $129,000; however, in my city of Santa Barbara, California, it is actually $117,000. Another great resource is www.infirmation.com/shared/insider/payscale.tcl (which has a lot of information about firms throughout the country and what they pay).

Who are the exceptions? Who is making the "big money" (above $200,000)? Some examples include the General Counsel for a hospital in Dallas, Texas ($330,000)[58] and David Stern, a graduate of Columbia, who is the third highest-paid sports

---

[56] http://volokh.com/2010/07/25/the-bimodal-distribution-of-lawyer-pay/.

[57] "The location of a school plays a big role in compensation for its graduates. Many of the schools that make our top 25 on mid-career pay are based in or around urban centers like New York and Boston or throughout California. The trade-off in these places, of course, is the higher cost of living." http://blogs.forbes.com/kurtbadenhausen/2011/03/08/the-best-law-schools-for-getting-rich/.

[58] www.dallasnews.com/news/community-news/dallas/headlines/20100914-parkland-hospital_s-top-lawyer-gets-year_s-salary-in-exit-package.ece.

commissioner ($10 million).[59] Right behind him is a graduate of
NYU, Gary Bettman, who made $7.2 million last year.[60] Equity
partners at BigLaw sometimes make $1 million per year.[61] It
is also important to keep in mind that some fields are more
lucrative than others. Patent work can be billed at high rates,
but many insurance defense attorneys have their rates capped in
the mid-$150 range per hour. Therefore, the insurance defense
attorney has to work a lot more hours to make the same money
as the patent attorney.

It is important to note that a full 75 percent of our survey
respondents (no matter how long they've been practicing law
or what kind of law they practice) agree with the statement, "I
feel that I can provide for myself and my family." I don't know
how many of the lawyers completed surveys from their yachts
in the Mediterranean, but I'm willing to go out on a limb and
say that—for most of us—that's not the standard of lifestyle we
reach for. (A pair of designer shoes now and then, that's more
reasonable.)[62]

---

[59] http://sports.yahoo.com/top/news?slug=ys-investopediacommish081310.

[60] Ibid.

[61] www.abajournal.com/magazine/article/the_secrets_of_million_dollar_solos/.

[62] Elvira Kras, my research assistant, asked me why I reach for designer shoes but not
for a designer law school. I think my flippant answer to her question is this: yes, the
outside world looks for the name brand of law schools and shoes and whatever they
can use to judge us most immediately. However, if I can afford my lovely YSL and
Jimmy Choos without having gone to a fancy law school, isn't that even more impressive? It is possible to pave your own way to success no matter where you go. The road
is arguably easier for my clients who graduate from Yale, Harvard, and Stanford, but
that's not the only way to live the designer lifestyle. I've read accounts of young associates at BigLaw who shop for designer shoes on the Internet because they can't leave
the office and who only wear their fancy shoes to work. That doesn't sound like much
fun to me. This was actually a pretty powerful metaphor in Jennifer Weiner's *In Her
Shoes* (a book made into a movie starring Toni Collette), about an attorney with no
time for a boyfriend or friends but who is very proud of the designer shoe collection
she never gets to wear, then gets upset with her sister for actually wearing them. But,
I digress from the topic at hand. The fact is that the "designer" schools are really only
available to a small portion of people, and those aren't the only people who should be

Keep in mind all of these positive things about being a lawyer and how lawyers feel about their lives and livelihoods because the next chapter may—and should, but only temporarily—deter you from pursuing your law school aspirations.

---

lawyers. There is a place for Uggs, Steve Maddens, and Nine West in the shoe world just as in the legal profession.

CHAPTER 6

OBJECTION!
TOO MANY LAWYERS, TOO MUCH DEBT, AND TOO FEW JOBS

HAVEN'T you heard? There are too many attorneys, law school is expensive, there are too few jobs, and the work is stressful with long hours. The message is getting out and the media is scrutinizing law schools closely.[63] A sampling of recent articles includes:

- "Is Law School a Losing Game" (coping with crushing law school debt in a depressed job market).[64]
- "A 45% Employment Rate? How Law School Employment Numbers Are Inflated " [65] and "Served: How Law Schools Completely Misrepresent Their Job Numbers" (showing how law schools fudge their

---

[63] College graduates and those with graduate degrees are also underemployed and unemployed. www.learnvest.com/money-tuneup/career/the-rising-cost-of-graduate-school-is-it-worth-it/; www.nytimes.com/2011/05/19/business/economy/19grads.html?_r=2&hp.

[64] www.nytimes.com/2011/01/09/business/09law.html.

[65] www.nationaljurist.com/
content/45-employment-rate-how-law-school-employment-numbers-are-inflated.

employment statistics for rankings and promotional purposes).[66]

- "Law Students Lose the Grant Game as Schools Win" (a *New York Times* article accusing law schools of not fully informing merit scholarship recipients about the likelihood that they will meet the grade point average requirement required by the terms of their scholarships).[67]

- "Law School Graduates Do Not Make $160,000" (a *Forbes* article taking a shot at how law schools report hiring data).[68]

- "Law School Loses Its Allure as Law Firm Jobs Are Scarce" (a *Wall Street Journal* Law Blog post about the downturn in law school applications in 2011 as compared to 2010, when people who couldn't find jobs hoped to ride out the recession in law school).[69]

Here are all (not a sampling, but *absolutely all*) of the negative comments we received from 258 attorneys who completed the survey regarding the current job market:

- "There is a surplus of entry-level lawyers that has built up over the last few years. Mid-size to BigLaw firms have gotten less willing to take on large numbers of new lawyers because they cannot work cost effectively and efficiently enough for clients' changing demands

---

[66] www.tnr.com/article/87251/
law-school-employment-harvard-yale-georgetown?page=0,1.

[67] www.nytimes.com/2011/05/01/business/law-school-grants.html.

[68] http://blogs.forbes.com/kurtbadenhausen/2011/03/23/
law-school-graduates-do-not-make-160000/.

[69] http://online.wsj.com/article/SB10001424052748704396504576204692878631
986.html.

for more economical legal services while still maintaining a high quality of work."

- "The blood bath of 2008–2009 will take years to shake out. There are too many attorneys already. Far too many kids enter law school to (1) save the world or (2) "work with people." There are other professions which are *far* better suited to those goals."

- "Law school is expensive and with the current market, the security and ease of employment is no longer the same. Attorney career satisfaction is also very low. Law school is definitely not for everyone and can be a *very* expensive investment. [People shouldn't attend] just because they can get into a good law school."

- There are "too many attorneys, too few jobs, too many jobs focused on pure billing and not on professional and personal growth."

Only one survey respondent passionately argued against law school without reservation. He graduated from Nova Southeastern School of Law in the last 6 to 10 years and weathered two layoffs from firms before opening his own practice.

Only go to law school if you *really* want to practice law. Statements such as 'a JD is more versatile than an MBA' are complete B.S. You go to law school to learn about legal theory, not how to run a business. Additionally, in spite of what you see on TV, practicing law really is a thankless job. All your clients think they know the law better than you; if you lose (through no fault of your own), clients wonder why they hired a lawyer in the first place since they wound up having to pay anyway; and if you win, clients wonder why they hired a lawyer because they didn't do anything wrong in the first place. Nowhere is this line of thinking more evident than the simple traffic ticket. I charge $100, which represents the time I have to spend driving to the courthouse and waiting for the case to be called. If I win because the cop doesn't show, clients think, 'Well, if I knew the cop wasn't going to show I would've gone myself and saved the $100.' If the police officer shows and you have to enter a plea, clients get upset because they think 'if I had known I would've been forced to pay the ticket I would've saved the money I spent on a lawyer and used that money toward the ticket.' Too many people go to law school because they don't know what they want to do with their life. My advice to them is this: before rushing off to three years of your life and tens of thousands of dollars in debt, work in a law firm for two years so you can see what it's like actually practicing law. If you don't like it, you only wasted a couple years and won't have to worry about the repayment of student loans. Also, the lawyer salary statistics are misleading. Yes, the top students at the top schools who get the BigLaw jobs in NYC and Washington will make big bucks, but if you're like 99 percent of the grads who didn't graduate in the top 10 percent of their class from a top school, depending on the city, if you're lucky enough to find a job in the first place, you might get offered a job for $36,000. Still wanna be a lawyer?

This response is similar to many postings on the Internet. I understand that a vocal, disgruntled population of young lawyers exists. I happen to believe that some people are negative no matter what, and that negativity comes through when they interview for jobs, network at events (if they go to the trouble of doing so), and interact with clients. I usually see a common thread in every disgruntled post I read—a complete lack of acknowledgment that there is anything the writer could have done better or differently. After all, a lawyer who is disgruntled can be reprimanded or terminated for his negative attitude; he could rub the firm's attorneys the wrong way by feeling entitled and bitter and affect the attorneys' attitude and work environment.

It is also important to keep in mind that lawyers are not alone in many of these feelings. Professionals of all kinds are at risk of becoming disenchanted. Doctors seek alternative ways of practicing medicine,[70] stockbrokers become high school basketball coaches[71]; there are books touting alternative careers for teachers[72] and scientists.[73] No profession is safe from people who enter it mistakenly, against their better judgment, because of parental pressure, or whose motivations change with age and maturity. There is a book for disgruntled PhD candidates about the uselessness of that degree.[74] An engineer I recently spoke with (whose father and brothers are also engineers) told me that neither he nor his brothers actually practice engineering, but their training in engineering taught them how to think. Just because law isn't a perfect profession, doesn't mean another one *is* perfect. You need to decide what the best option is for you,

---

[70] www.medicalcareerchange.com/.

[71] www.depauw.edu/ath/news/story/16759/.

[72] www.amazon.com/101-Career-Alternatives-Teachers-Opportunities/dp/0761534520 and www.amazon.com/Alternative-Careers-Science-Scientific-Survival/dp/0125893760/ref=sr_1_1?s=books&ie=UTF8&qid=130387254 6&sr=1-1.

[73] Ibid.

[74] www.amazon.com/PhD-Not-Enough-Survival-Science/dp/0465022227/ref=pd_luc_top_sim_00_02_t_lh.

and go into it knowing that every day isn't going to be rosy and ideal. Everybody has bad days, even people who never went to law school.

For all of the people who say there are no jobs, I point to the local bar newsletters and Twitter feeds that say otherwise. I hear of people getting hired as entry-level lawyers all the time. My husband's office has five attorneys, hired two new attorneys this year (and will hire another pending passage of the bar exam), and are always looking for people in their other offices. Most of us have to begin our careers in monotonous, paper-pushing, jobs, but some attorneys do get to start out their careers with autonomy on a caseload, making appearances in court and handling trials by themselves, interacting with clients, and getting a car allowance. The offices might not be fancy, but what good are fancy offices when you are mired in document review and memo writing? Yet, many law grads don't apply for these jobs because the starting salaries are lower, and they have significant loans to pay back. Just in case you are tempted to think that this is just one example, I urge you to look at legal newspapers and websites in your geographic area and see who is hiring lawyers and what they are being hired to do. Legal recruiting websites are another good source of information. Knowing where the jobs are and exploring now whether you would be happy working in those jobs will enable you to make a better decision about whether to enter the legal field.

CHAPTER 7

HINDSIGHT:
WOULD LAWYERS MAKE
DIFFERENT CHOICES?

O NE of the benefits of having more than 250 lawyers fill out a survey is so that you can learn from their mistakes. I wanted to know what they felt, in hindsight, was most important about choosing a law school. This information is vital not only because they have the perspective that comes with years of experience, but because these are the people who will be hiring you when you graduate from law school. Let's take a look at what is important to them.

Where Would They Attend Law School?

Figure 7.1 gives detailed statistics with the lawyers' responses to the question, *In what order of importance would you rank each of these considerations in choosing a law school to attend?*

Figure 7.1 **In what order of importance would you rank each of these considerations in choosing a law school to attend?**

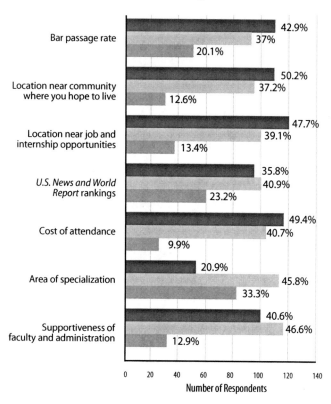

Comments regarding other important considerations included:

- "Support for public interest."
- "A school's history in the community (city, state, or country) was very important for me."
- "Alumni network of the law school and the effectiveness of the placement office."
- "Honesty of the school regarding the career and your prospects within it."

- "Ability to volunteer in field while attending law school."
- "Yale is just a unique place—an experience like no other."
- "Where the school is located is important in terms of finding peace and tranquility in an otherwise intense and hectic law school world."
- "I looked at the percentage of recent graduates in the public and nonprofit sector."
- "I recommend people attend law school in the city they hope to practice in and, if there are multiple cities they are willing to work in, then the city with the greatest need for the type of lawyer the student hopes to become."

How Much Would They Spend on Law School?

Lawyers and prospective lawyers rank things about the same when choosing to attend a law school, with one very major exception. Although only 54 percent of those contemplating law school ranked cost as being an important or very important factor in choosing a law school, *it was far and away the most important factor* that lawyers would urge you to consider. In fact, 90 percent of the lawyers marked cost as being somewhat or very important.

When I graduated from law school, I had $55,000 in law school loans. At first, the $800/month payments were stifling: after all, I made $34,000 in 1999. There may even have been a few months when I deferred payments, but I've blocked that out from my memory. The next year, I got a job paying $75,000 and consolidated my loans and locked in an interest rate that was half of the original rate. After that, my loans stopped being something I thought about very often. I'll probably pay them off in full by the end of this year, but only because I'll choose to pay them off eight years early and not because it was a stretch to do so. Therefore, as I read accounts of recent law school graduates who get divorced over the stress of mutual law school loan debt, I felt strongly about telling the world that—yes—this is tough at first but it gets better, and it gets better quickly.[75] Of the lawyers we surveyed, 52 percent are still repaying law school loans—that's 135 people (83 people already paid off their loans and 40 did not take out loans). Of the 135, 78 said that their law school loans impact their career and life choices. Of these, 75 percent were within 10 years of law school graduation.

Many of the lawyers who completed our survey included the cost of attendance as part of their response to whether they would recommend that others attend law school. For example, Noelle Hale, a graduate of Pepperdine states,

> I am glad that I went to law school and think that it has benefited me immeasurably in both my personal and professional lives. However, I had the extremely good fortune of having assistance with paying for law school and, therefore, do not have student loans. I do tell people who are considering law school today that they need to take a very realistic look at the legal market and make a smart decision if they have no other choice than to take out more than $100,000 in loans. I work with law students because I work with a bar review company, and I see the distress that so many of them are in as they graduate with such considerable debt and no job offers.

---

[75] www.forbes.com/forbes/2009/0202/060.html.

One corporate transactional attorney who makes "significantly more" than the median of $105,000 says that his student loans still dictate his career and life choices. "Unless one meets the criteria to attend a top-ranked law school or will not need to worry about paying for tuition, law school is a huge financial burden that many underestimate. The financial burden can often dictate your career and certain personal decisions." Austin Groothuis, who graduated from Chicago Kent in 2008, said that if you really want to be a lawyer you need to fit into one or more of the following four categories:

1. You or your family are independently wealthy and can pay for law school and cost of living during law school without, or with very few, loans.
2. You have been given a scholarship to your school, guaranteed or very likely to be renewed, which will pay for all or most of law school and cost of living without, or with very few, loans.
3. You get into a Top 10 to 15 or so school.
4. You have a relative or someone similar who can guarantee you a job after law school.
    Only then would I recommend law school.

Austin proves my point: There's not a lot of harm in going to law school if you're not paying for it. You might have parents willing to foot the bill, or you might be able to get a scholarship from a law school that would be happy to play the *U.S. News and World Report* rankings by attracting someone with your LSAT score and GPA. Of course, you have to read the fine print about any scholarship you accept because it might not be easily renewed in the last two years of law school.[76]

---

[76] www.nytimes.com/2011/05/01/business/law-school-grants.html.

One of my former law school classmates, Kira Willig, offered this explanation,

> I chose to attend the University of Miami School of Law in part because they gave me a full scholarship. It allowed me to pursue my chosen field of family law, where my starting salary was about one-third of that of my fellow graduates. It has paid off enormously as my interest in family law led to my current position as an adjunct professor of family law at the University of Miami. I was able to pay off all of my college, law school [living expenses] and bar loans just a few years out of law school, and get to practice an area of law I am passionate about.

Law schools are trying to educate students regarding these issues. Nancy Levit, co-author of *The Happy Lawyer* and a faculty member at University of Missouri-Kansas City, says,

> We talk about availability of loan repayment assistance programs (school and state sponsored programs to help graduates who choose lower paying public interest careers) and public interest/public service careers, and being in one of these jobs is correlated with job satisfaction. Usually you are able to live your ideals in these jobs. A number of law schools offer flexible scheduling or part-time programs and may not advertise them for people who need to work their way through. It would be valuable to find out which law schools have part-time/flex programs. You have to complete the education in five years, but if people need to juggle, these may be options.

The law school where she is a faculty member also provides programs during Orientation to help new students keep these issues in mind. "We have a one-hour session on how to make a budget and stick to it during law school so you don't live outside your means during law school and have to pay for it the rest of your life."

It's not just solo practitioners and public interest attorneys who have more options because they took scholarships to law school. Noah Solomon, Vice President of Legal Affairs at BBC, attended Southwestern because he would graduate without significant debt. As a result, when he decided to enter the field of entertainment law, he had the flexibility to spend a year as someone's assistant in hopes of being promoted later on. "Southwestern was free and that was the deciding factor," he said. "The benefit of having minimal loans is that it allowed me to look at every possibility. I knew I did not want to work in a firm and I didn't feel like I had to; I could take a job that paid less out of school because it was something I wanted to do." (It worked, by the way, and for more about Noah's career in entertainment law, see Chapter 15.)

Current 2L Elyssa Tannenbaum says she feels taking a scholarship to George Washington was the best thing she could have done because it made all of her other decisions very easy— she feels free to make mistakes, try things to see what she likes, and doesn't feel the need to pigeonhole herself into a career at the age of 23. A 2L at Rutgers, Nicole Ganci, agrees: "I knew I didn't want to work in public interest after graduation, but I also I knew I didn't want to rack up debt too big to wrap my head around—attending a state university on scholarship allows me to have access to opportunity without the six-figure debt."

Would They Choose a Different Practice Area?

For all of the buzz about the importance of choosing an area of law to practice, most lawyers are not practicing in their intended areas (69 percent), but 74 percent of lawyers we surveyed would stay in their same area of law practice. This is a surprisingly positive statistic—the grass is not always greener. For the remainder, reasons for wanting to change included:

- "I would like to add a practice area—something paid on an hourly basis to minimize the ups and downs of a contingency fee practice" (contributed by a graduate of Columbia who has more than 15 years' experience in law and is the managing partner of her own law firm).
- "Financial remuneration" (said by a recent graduate of a top 25 school who is working as an assistant district attorney).
- "Boredom, not fulfilling; cynical" (said by a recent graduate currently working in a temporary contract placement whose overall survey results are very down on law school)."The market is oversaturated; the profession on the whole is unfulfilling and typi- cally creates cynicism about your fellow man. Ninety percent of all litigation involves MONEY. Law schools offer NO real-world experience while selling the illusion of career satisfaction and a comfortable career. Law schools selling the pipe dream and admit- ting anyone who can get a loan is the main problem."
- "I turned down offers for jobs I thought would be boring but would have been more lucrative and

> maybe would have led to more job/financial security,
> but I didn't know it because of lack of guidance."

Finding the right area of law is an important part of the exploration process. One lawyer stated that her stress level lessened tremendously once she found the right area of law. "I am at a happy place in my career now, but I see so many lawyers who are not. It has taken me 10 plus years to get a handle on the stress. I still get 'stressed out' over cases at times, but I've adapted to it somewhat. I've finally found an area of law that I enjoy practicing." For more about how to decide on a practice area, see Chapter 17, "Choosing an Area of Specialization."

PART III

A LIFE IN LAW

The more lawyers there are, the more people are out there to encourage others not to go to law school.

David E. Kelley, television
screenwriter and producer

CHAPTER 8

UNDERSTANDING WHY LAWYERS WORK SO HARD

LAWYERS basically get paid in one of four ways: salary, contingency, billable hour, or flat-fee services.

Salary

Public employees and public interest attorneys are paid by a salary seniority step ladder system. There usually isn't much negotiating leverage: you just have to put in the time. In-house counsel salaries are based on experience level, merit, the size of the organization, and what the market bears. However, if you're earning a salary at a law firm, it is also based on the number of hours you are expected to bill, and you probably will be on a bonus structure for additional hours billed or total amounts billed that are above a certain threshold (see billable hour discussion below).

Contingency

Plaintiff attorneys, who represent people with personal injury, civil rights, insurance claims, etc., will often make a percentage of what is collected on behalf of their clients. This means that you don't always get paid, and sometimes you will want to settle cases rather than take them through an expensive trial that forces you to forgo other work and, perhaps, puts you at odds with what your client wants to do. It makes your lifestyle unpredictable but also allows you to have some very big years if you take on the most promising cases, including class actions.

Billable Hour

Most of private practice, and almost all of private practice defense work, is based on the billable hour. Some attorneys bill at $150/hour (remember—a big chunk of this goes to pay overhead, including paralegals, administrative assistants, and offices) and some bill at $1,000; however, most attorneys bill in the $200 to $400 range per hour. If you work for yourself, the number of hours you bill is how you make your money, and you make even more money if you have other lawyers billing hours on your behalf (since you keep the profits after paying overhead, which includes their salaries). This is why being an equity partner in a firm is the way to really make money while practicing law—if you own a piece of overall profit, then you are making money while other people are working in addition to making money off the hours you are billing personally. If associates are making big money, it has to come from somewhere: equity partners are unlikely to give up their take, and clients are unlikely to want to pay higher billable hours. The result is the conflicting and dangerous area where the number of hours billed and the demanding lifestyle that comes with it collide. We discuss the ramifications of this further in the next chapter.

However, there are downsides to the billable hour. The most obvious is that to bill a lot of hours you have to WORK a lot of hours. Of our survey respondents, 50 percent bill hours. Among those attorneys:

- 15% bill between 0 to 1,500 hours annually
- 8% bill between 1,501 to 1,800 hours annually
- 14% bill between 1,801 to 2,000 hours annually
- 10% bill between 2,001 to 2,500 hours annually
- 3% bill between 2,501 to 3,000 hours annually

Only one person billed between 3,001 to 3,500 hours and only two people billed more than 3,500 hours a year. (I'm fairly certain one of those was my husband and the other was his partner. They are both crazy workaholics, worked equally crazy hours in their careers prior to law school, and both had fathers who were litigators. The irony is that my husband was a caterer and went to law school at age 27 because he wanted a job where the hours were more reasonable and the work was less physically demanding.) To bill 2,000 hours a year, you must bill 40 hours per week if you take two weeks of vacation. At 2,500 hours, you are billing 50 hours per week.

When evaluating this breakdown, remember that not every hour at work can be billed—there are meetings to attend, office issues to manage, financial issues to oversee, water cooler conversation to partake in, and personnel crises that require intervention. Therefore, when asked how many hours a week they currently work, our responders answered as illustrated in Figure 8.1.

Figure 8.1 **How many hours a week do you currently work?**

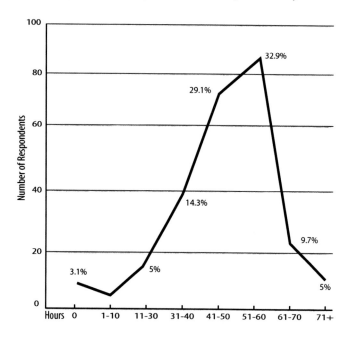

If you want to know what it really means to work 60 hours a week, see Derek Roberti's description in *Should I Go to Law School: The $100,000 Gamble* (New York: R + S Media, 2011).[77] JDBliss.com also offers a work/life balance calculator.[78]

While searching online for "happy lawyer," I came across a great speech by Stephen C. Ellis, an attorney and managing partner of Tucker, Ellis & West. He gave this address in 2008 to the graduating class at Case Western Reserve School of Law in Cleveland, Ohio, his alma mater. In this speech, he outlines the lessons he learned as managing partner of a law firm with 500

---

[77] See pages 36 and 37.

[78] www.envoyglobal.net/jdbliss/test/calculator2.htm.

attorneys that went out of business. He talks about how 200 of the lawyers stuck together and built a new firm where associates were judged on the quality of their work rather than on the number of hours billed and the amount of money made.[79] I highly suggest reading it in its entirety for a worthwhile perspective on building a law practice.

New trends in the legal marketplace are emerging that might see a slide away from the traditional billable hour model. Deborah Epstein Henry says "There's a lot of pressure on the billable hour model. There is momentum because the economic downturn put pressure on the model in a way that never existed, and clients became a lot more sophisticated and wanted firms to share the risk." She is seeing a significant change toward using alternative fees and firms feeling pressure to revisit the way they bill for their work. "Another change I'm seeing is a shrinkage of associate classes because of shrinking demand for legal services across the board (because work is being outsourced and clients are more sophisticated about using nonlawyer professionals) and also because clients will no longer pay for junior lawyer training." She says that firms are not going to be able to bill out less-experienced lawyers at the same rates as in the past, and more firms will raise rates only after lawyers have achieved certain competencies like having a certain number of depositions or motions for summary judgment under their belts, or having closed a certain number of deals.[80]

Scott Carter is Executive Vice President and General Counsel for Franklin Street Properties in Massachusetts. He is concerned that the current legal job market may become the

---

[79] http://davidmaister.com/blog/602/Being-a-Happy-and-Successful-Lawyer.

[80] Interview, 06/22/2011.

new "normal." "BigLaw has dramatically reduced hiring both summer associate and permanent associate positions, and I am not sure when or if they will return to old hiring levels. Long gone are the days of law firms courting law students with extravagant summer activities and social events." He has also seen changes in how law firms charge their clients. "Also, as a general counsel, the majority of the work that I send to BigLaw is done on a fixed-fee basis, so in my view the billable hour, although still alive, is becoming far less common."

Flat-Fee Service

As mentioned above, a newly emerging trend in private practice is flat-fee billing. Although some insurance companies have mandated that their attorneys bill this way, more small business clients are opting for this kind of billing. Kevin Houchin, who is a solo practitioner and author of *Fuel the Spark: 5 Guiding Values for Success in Law School & Beyond* (New York: Morgan James Publishing, 2009) and the article, "Confessions of a Happy Lawyer,"[81] swears by it. He offers clients three choices ($375/month, $750/month, and $1500/month). For more information about how this method is implemented and why, see http://lawyerist.com/flat-fee-billing-set-you-free/.

How Demanding Is the Practice of Law?

No matter how much (or how little) money they make, lawyers work hard. Of the lawyers who responded, 80 percent stated that "a willingness to work hard" is the most important trait for success in their careers. If you are a "traditional" law

---

[81] http://lawyerist.com/confessions-of-a-happy-lawyer/.

school applicant (still in college or within a year or two of graduation), then you might not be accustomed to thinking about family life except in the context of visiting your parents and getting a free dinner out once in a while. However, the day will probably come when you have your own family and that changes your willingness to spend every waking minute at work. Although it's impossible to look into the future, you can plan for it by making career choices that leave things like a family life open for consideration. To help you do this, here are some results from our survey that you should be aware of:

- 67% of survey responders say they usually work one or more weekend days per month. Here is the breakdown:
  - 35% usually work one to two weekend days per month
  - 22% usually work three to five weekend days per month
  - Only 10% usually work more than five weekend days per month
  - 63% see their family all together and awake at least three nights per week

If you are willing to put in the time, you are likely to reap rewards. A full 64 percent stated, "My career provides a good quality of life;" 43 percent stated, "My career allows time for a rich personal life" and "My career allows me to focus on my health, family, and spiritual needs." Only 46 percent said "My career enables me to be a good spouse/parent" (of course, people may not have checked this as an option if they were single and without kids, things that our survey did not ask about), and only 35 percent said "I feel that I take vacations often enough" (but that might just be the American way of life).

On our survey, 39 percent of respondents said they are under a great deal of stress. This stress can lead to serious problems.

Harvey Hyman, who posts 10 Maxims for being a Happier, Healthier Lawyer (including meditating and performing acts of random kindness daily), states on his website:

> There are nearly 1.2 million lawyers in the United States. Twenty percent of them suffer from major depression or alcoholism. This is much higher than the rates of major depression (6.5 percent) or alcoholism (10 percent) in society at large. Lawyers are 3.6 times more likely to be depressed than all other persons generally employed full time. They have the highest rate of divorce among all occupational groups and are near the top of the suicide list. Surveys show that more than half of all lawyers would quit their field and try something new if not prevented from doing so by economics. As it now exists, law practice generates levels of stress, misery, mental illness, and substance abuse that are both shocking and unacceptable.[82]

Of course, how you deal with problems and stressors now (without being a lawyer) can give you a good indication of whether you'll be able to deal with the pressures of being a lawyer. For example, if you are someone who gets sick when you are stressed out, who has trouble keeping up with school and/or work when you are very busy, or who already turns to alcohol when things get rough, then you may want to really think about whether this is the profession that is most conducive to your continuing mental health. Some people can take it and I admit I am one of them. Just in the course of one month, I moved

---

[82] http://lawyerswellbeing.com/maxims.html.

houses (and unpacked all of the boxes and put everything away within two days), handled two real estate transactions, worked with clients, ran a business, took care of my husband and daughters, played tennis three times a week, and traveled across the country to meet my new niece. I was the same way as an undergrad (working part time, getting good grades, serving as president of two student organizations at once, etc.) and in law school (working at least 20 hours a week while ranking at the top of my class and taking on leadership roles on campus). This is just the way I've always been. I know I can handle a lot more than most people (preparing me especially well to run my own business). If you have difficulty with this, then you may want to reconsider law school. However, if you thrive on being busy and feeling important, there are ways to balance the demands of the profession with the hours and still live a nice lifestyle.

One attorney who responded to our survey showed how attitude about stress makes all the difference. He said, "My stress is the good kind—I absolutely LOVE what I do and I'm in high demand so my days are very full. At the same time, my office is 30 feet from my back door and I am tremendously involved in the lives of my (homeschooled) children and my beautiful wife." If you have trouble handling stress or you're not sure how you would do under this kind of pressure, spend some time working full time while studying for the LSAT and see how you cope.

CHAPTER 9

THE BUSINESS OF LAW

Lawyers As Entrepreneurs

FOR lawyers in private practice, law is their business. If what you really want to do is run a major corporation, then a law degree can get you there. However, it probably isn't the most direct route. According to headhunting firm Spencer Stuart, only 10.8 percent of the CEOs of companies in the Standard & Poor's 500-stock index have law degrees. A recent Businessweek.com article stated that lawyers are often seen as ineffective business directors, but that generalization has been disproven by a chosen few, including Kenneth I. Chenault of American Express and Richard D. Parsons of Time Warner.[83]

How much of being a successful attorney depends on being a savvy business person? According to our survey, 32 percent of lawyers cited "business experience prior to attending law school" as being one of the experiences that assisted them in their current career. Whether you end up in the executive suite or not, business knowledge is helpful in most areas of law because, after all, law is a way of making money; the smarter you are at making money and at helping your clients make

---

[83] www.businessweek.com/magazine/content/04_50/b3912101_mz056.htm.

money, the more successful you will be. That's where business sense comes in to play.

According to Kimberly K. Egan of DLA Piper:

> BigLaw firms' most successful rainmakers can carry on a conversation with anyone about anything, even if they are bored stiff doing it. This skill is sometimes known as "cocktail party conversation." Reading the newspaper in the morning is a good habit for new associates to develop. Reading the front section and the business section, at a minimum, and one local paper and one national paper in addition to at least one general-interest publication helps lawyers discuss cultural issues of the moment with colleagues and clients.[84]

In addition, whether as an associate trying to become partner or as an equity partner in a firm, having your own clients makes the difference in your career trajectory (of counsel or partner) and income (typically the value of one-third of billable hours for the rest of your life, or the potential to bring in business and have enough work for several attorneys and make money from them as well). This is where developing an entrepreneurial mindset is essential. Mona Stone, Of Counsel with Greenberg Traurig in Phoenix, Arizona, graduated from Tulane in 1997 and was listed in "Top 40 Illinois Attorneys under 40 to Watch" in the *Chicago Daily Law Bulletin* (2008). She has also authored three books, including *Future Performance: Your Guide to a Successful Career in Law* (Boston: Aspatore Books, a division of Thomson Reuters, 2009). In a phone interview with

---

[84] www.law.com/jsp/nlj/PubArticleNLJ.jsp?id=1202483306319&slreturn=1&hbxl ogin=1; February 8, 2011.

me she stressed the importance of business savvy in building your career trajectory:

> Young lawyers need to be assertive and be self-promoters. Law school does not do an adequate job of teaching the business of being a lawyer. It's very abstract and theoretical, but private practitioners need to—within 3 to 5 years—start establishing connections and building a client base. More and more, it's critical for a young lawyer at a private law firm to understand the importance of business development, marketing, and self-promotion. It's important to bring in clients who match the values of the firm—at a big firm we charge top rates for top service; clients need to be able to pay. Young lawyers need to understand the financial aspect of it.
>
> It's got to be about self-promotion. I have a roster in my book and keep logs of speaking engagements and publications. This is an easy way to self-promote. One way to show you have a special skill set that other attorneys don't is to publish articles and speak, even if you're just assisting a senior lawyer in the beginning. If you're a litigator, keep track of the cases you've handled and say what success you had and what value you added that led to a good outcome. When it comes time for a self-evaluation or to talk to clients or prospective clients, you can say what you accomplished. This is important within your organization, too—you have to market what you are doing.
>
> When I published my most recent book on EEOC, I e-mailed the entire firm and got positive feedback,

and attorneys at the firm said it would be a great client gift. I am getting my name out there and saying I have a special skill level in handling EEOC claims.

You also have to know what your colleagues' strengths are and keep track of it. Have an elevator pitch and detailed firm bio—all of these things go to your individual brand and marketing.

More than ever, large firms just expect as an unwritten rule that you produce high-caliber work and you'll make a decent salary. But, how much work are you originating and cross-selling? "Did Mona bring in an estate planning matter, a bankruptcy matter?" The more I feed my colleagues as well as myself, the more successful I will be. Make your network as big as possible. With social media, Facebook, and LinkedIn, younger attorneys can really maximize different ways of marketing and capitalize on them.[85]

Of course, it takes time to cultivate your own clients. Brandon Scheele told me about his experience as a young lawyer:

As a young lawyer, the most frustrating thing I remember was that nobody respects you at the beginning no matter how good you were. Peers and bosses do, but clients don't. [It's] nearly impossible for a young lawyer to get clients. You have to have a few gray hairs or years before people really start trusting you and thinking of *you* as their lawyer as opposed to *your supervisor*. The more experience you get, the more you get involved in real responsibility and

---

not just research and writing (the more you are doing depositions and trying cases); that's when you get the respect and that's when you start getting clients and not until then. It's important to find a firm that allows you to do this stuff right from the beginning otherwise you're not going to get clients. You need to get real experience early and often so they start to think of you as the lawyer and not your supervisor.

Chris Kratovil, also a partner in a large firm, admits there are a lot of lawyers all chasing the same limited body of work in commercial litigation while trying to differentiate themselves from their competition. "Bringing in new business is the hardest part; however, it's not so different from any other field."[86]

Here is an example: my small town has five frozen yogurt shops. Five. Three are on the same street. Where to go comes down to price, service, product, and location. Law isn't much different. For lawyers who want to avoid this atmosphere, a new trend is arising—at-home legal jobs with no rainmaking or billing required.[87]

Deborah Epstein Henry[88] emphasized to me the importance of being your own entrepreneur and charting your own path.

The historic notion of law is that it is a gentlemen's profession with a senior lawyer carving your path for you, but for the most part that doesn't exist anymore. I ask all prospective lawyers, "Are you willing to take the

---

[86] Interview with Elvira Kras, 04/25/2011.

[87] www.abajournal.com/news/article/
legal_entrepreneur_forms_dc_law_firm_that_shuns_office_face_time_and_lawyer/.

[88] Interview on 06/30/2011; see also Deborah Epstein Henry, *Law & Reorder: Legal Industry Solutions for Restructure, Retention, Promotion & Work/Life Balance* (Chicago: American Bar Association, 2010).

initiative and be an entrepreneur and assume control of your career?" Because that's what's required for lawyers to succeed today. It used to be if you were smart and hardworking and a top-notch lawyer, that's all you needed. Now it's an assumption that you're good and talented, and the lawyers who are thriving have additional components to their profile.

She offers five such components (which I've paraphrased slightly and which are more fully discussed in her book)[89]:

1. Leadership skills.
2. Flexibility.
3. Networking.
4. Ability to develop relationships with people in your life who can endorse you and open opportunities for you.
5. Ability to focus on your own career development and promotion by knowing who you have to work with and what matters you need to be staffed on to climb up the ladder.

I completely agree with this. I am in a nontraditional legal career (I have not practiced law since 2005), but I hustle every single day to make sure my thriving business remains thriving. My husband is a partner in a law firm that has offices throughout California, and he still hustles for files and travels to "market" his abilities and his firm to prospective and current clients. When an insurance adjuster moves from one company to another, he makes sure to keep that contact alive and work to get on the list of attorneys used by the new company. If all he did was bill his hours and keep his head down, he wouldn't be a partner. He

---

[89] Interview on 06/30/2011.

would run out of work. There is no one else generating work to support him and his secretary—it's his responsibility to do that. He understood that from day one (after all, his father was also an insurance defense attorney). I learned to be an entrepreneur from my husband, and it's the most valuable thing I've learned. Because I have a law degree and because I know how to make money for myself, I know I will always be ok. I won't need anyone else to hand me a job (see Chapter 11 for more on being your own boss).

Do You Need an MBA to Be a Lawyer?

When I was working in private practice, I felt behind the game because I did not have a business background but found myself spending considerable time and effort scouring clients' financials and profit and loss reports in preparation for litigation. Law school applicants often ask me whether they should pursue a joint JD/MBA to make themselves more marketable and/or to add to their experiences. In our survey, only 14 percent felt that a graduate degree in a field other than law was an experience that assisted them in their careers. We did not specifically ask about an MBA or how many respondents had an MBA, but we can infer from this response that it is a rather small percentage of attorneys who also hold an MBA.

Bobby Pearce was one of those few with both degrees. He attended the University of South Carolina for his JD/MBA, and more than 20 years has passed since his graduation. Although the program took him four years, including summers, in his interview with us he said it was

> . . .the best decision I ever made in business; it gave me two career paths and has really worked out to be

two careers meshed into one. I came out of law and business school and went into the business world doing transactions advising small companies, small management consulting, merger and acquisition work; but my work frequently bled over into legal world, first using my legal education for 20 percent of my work then flip-flopping when I joined a law firm where I was doing 80 percent legal work, but 20 percent of my knowledge came from my business background.

He says having his MBA proved to be a huge asset.

Very few lawyers know how to run a business, and having an MBA is a big advantage when you are talking with a corporate client. It is a big advantage to be able to read a balance sheet, to be able to understand manufacturing logistics—it gives you a completely different perspective and adds credibility when working with corporate clients. Having a JD/MBA doubled the opportunities that I had.

Bobby provides advice for those who hope to follow in his footsteps.

If you do get into the business world or legal world, try and focus on getting the most broad-based experience that you can. Do not try to find the one place or area that makes the most money. Dedicate the first five years to getting the most broad-based experience, ask for work, tell them you will do anything, make sure to get experience and knowledge in different areas, rather than getting stuck in a very narrow market. That way you will be a tremendous asset for the rest of your working career.

Jasper Kim, associate professor and department chair at

Ewha Womens University in Korea, says having more than one graduate degree made him more marketable in a number of career paths.

> Law school made me what I am today. But in today's globalized world, the JD degree can no longer be the end-all-be-all. It must be complemented with other on-demand skill sets like languages, IT skills, or another area of "technical" expertise. For example, in my case, I have a JD and an MSc (from the London School of Economics) in addition to being able to speak both English and Korean. This opens up some opportunities in terms of industry (law and finance/economics/business) and region (North America, EU, and Asia).

There are, of course, a few reasons *not* to pursue a joint degree (MBA or otherwise). First, there is the added expense and added time; there is also the possibility of lost prospects and opportunities because you could have spent that time working or doing additional activities to help further your career in law. Also, it can be difficult socially to switch back and forth between programs and groups of friends, and it's hard to maintain connections with faculty and administration at both schools. Sometimes the schools might not even be located on the same campus. Plus, it can make you appear unfocused to employers—hedging your bets between career options or being truly undecided about what you want to do with your life. To overcome this possible objection, you will want to constantly keep this issue at the forefront of your mind and actively incorporate law into your business curriculum and vice versa. If you are taking mostly gender studies courses at the law school and finance at the business school, you might have some explaining to do.

One JD/MBA student at Rutgers told me there were these potential drawbacks:

- The main critique I hear is that some employers will frown on the dual-degree because it demonstrates a lack of commitment to the law.
- Also, sometimes people ask me if I feel like I've forgotten all the material from 1L having spent the past year entirely at the business school.
- Additionally, people sometimes ask why I chose to pursue the degree and how it fits into my career goals. A career counselor at the business school (who did not know I was a dual degree) told me how asinine he thinks the combination is and how most people getting it don't have a clear sense of why they are doing it.
- Other critiques I have heard indicate that a dual degree is only worthwhile at a Top 10 school OR at law schools with equally good or better business programs.

The takeaway: think before you do. An extra year of school may not pay itself back in dividends. Only pursue this if you are dedicated to a career in business and/or business law and have talked to people who hire for positions you hope to hold one day to find out what they think. If the results are mixed, consider that it might just be a way to demonstrate business acumen for those who lack real-world business experience.

CHAPTER 10

THE ALLURE OF BIGLAW

MOST of the press about law careers and lawyer salaries is really about the biggest law firms, affectionately named BigLaw. There are a lot of reasons for this. Of course, that's where recent law school graduates make the most money. In turn, it's where law schools would most like to place their graduates (to help their *U.S. News and World Report* rankings and attract more tuition-paying students, thereby attracting more BigLaw employers to their students, etc.).[90]

Many law school applicants make decisions about where to attend law school based on where they feel they would be most likely to be hired by BigLaw. When I was in law school, one friend told me he was taking a BigLaw job just until he could pay off his loans, and then he was going to work in a public interest field. I tried searching for him online but can't find any indication of whether he followed through on this plan. Another told me he planned to work at BigLaw, become a partner, and retire by age 47 (he's well on his way as of this printing). Yet another classmate stayed with BigLaw for seven years before joining the general counsel's office of a large federal agency.

---

[90] www.7thcircuitbar.org/associations/1507/files/Circuit%20Rider%20Vol%2010.pdf.

I had no BigLaw aspirations. I entered law school with the intention of working for the government or plaintiff side of employment discrimination matters. Because my grades placed me near the top of my class, my career services office steered me heavily toward the BigLaw firms in their employment defense sections. What happened? I spent my summer clerking for two large firms, was pretty miserable because I didn't know how to play the game, and entered my third year without any job offers. Apparently, I'm not the only victim of this phenomenon. "A significant aspect of what I refer to as the 'funneling' of as high as 95 percent of the graduates at selective law schools to large law firms through on-campus interviewing is that as many as 50 percent of the students wanted careers serving the public and were diverted from those careers," according to Ronald Fox, who assists lawyers with career planning.[91]

Brandon Scheele, who took the BigLaw path and looks for it when hiring people for his firm, told me:

> When you get to law school, you need good grades to get interviewed by big firms. That's what I wanted to do. I graduated at the top of my class, got a big firm job, and was flown all over the state and wined and dined. I started a new firm two years ago and split off, but I was with the biggest law firm in the state [for many years]. It was pretty laid back. We didn't work ourselves to death. Starting in a big firm opens a lot of doors for you. The sheer level of lawyers you're interacting with and the social events and community involvement allows you to meet so many more people than if you're working with two or three lawyers. And it looks

---

[91] www.lawyersatisfactionblog.com/2009/11/will-college-students-continue.html.

good on a resume if you are coming from a nationally recognized law firm. People know you worked really hard and you were good enough and you did it. It's a rite of passage, a feather in your cap. I advocate for that path because I think it works. I'm in an 85-lawyer firm right now. When hiring, if we want someone with experience, that path is still what we look for. I just hired someone a month ago to work for me, and I wouldn't interview someone who wasn't in the top 20 percent of their class. Also, if I saw someone coming from Holland & Knight or another big firm, that would impress me. If we want someone with experience with research, writing, and handling depositions, I prefer that path.

Martha Kimes, intellectual property law counsel for GoDaddy.com and author of *Ivy Briefs: True Tales of a Neurotic Law Student* (Atria Books/Simon & Schuster, 2007) says that in addition to the obvious advantages of working for BigLaw,

> You are exposed to things that people are really impressed by. It's a springboard that gives you a lot of opportunities you wouldn't otherwise have or at least not have so easily. It's not necessarily because being in BigLaw positions you uniquely with skills you might not otherwise have; people are impressed that you're working on deals that are in the headlines and you've worked for Fortune 100 companies and it makes an impression. A giant difference between BigLaw and working in-house is the resources you have available. As a young lawyer (at BigLaw) you're not constrained by how much time you spend on Westlaw because of client billing issues—in-house is a lot more quick and

dirty; but in the law firm, people are paying you to look in every nook and cranny and give well-thought-out answers to things. It's a great way to learn how to be a lawyer. By the very nature of BigLaw, there are so many people that it increases your chances of finding someone who can be a mentor to you. You have more people at your disposal to help you think about where you want to go. Once you've been in BigLaw, you're in the club. You may not want to stay in the club, but having been in it, it doesn't go away.[92]

I recently spoke to a second year associate at Cravath, Swain & Moore in New York City (the crème de la crème of white shoe NYC law firms). He isn't sure what his next career step will be, or whether he will continue to practice law. I let him know that just because *this* way of practicing law wasn't appealing to him in the long run, another way of practicing might be a perfect fit. Attorney Bobby Pearce likens it to finding the "porridge that is just right"—some will be too hot for you, some too cold, but experimenting and finding the right place is essential.

Bobby, who spent 12 years with a law firm of about 440 lawyers, and now practices in a 170-person law firm, explains it this way:

In the management of BigLaw firms, the focus is on numbers and the collection rate of each attorney incentivizes lawyers to hoard the work and turns into a great deal of competition internally within the law firm over clients, over collections, and over credit. BigLaw is a big business. What occurs is an isolating effect of small teams within the law firm; with 500 to 600 lawyers, it is impossible to know all the lawyers and, therefore, the work loses the partnership feeling. What I tried to do is to look around for a long time at smaller firms, at solo practice, 40-person firms; it made so much sense to go down to a size of firm that really provided flexibility and teamwork and balance and congeniality. I did a lot of research to find the right fit. [One factor for me is that I believe] the individual bonus system destroys camaraderie and congeniality, and it is better to want to make the pie bigger, not just your slice of the pie bigger. The firm has shown that they will pay you for what you are good at, will reward you for what you are good at—be it management or sitting at the desk—because each person brings something different to the table and they are small enough to recognize that people need to be rewarded for what they are good at. If you individually want to make a lot of money, then you should look at BigLaw because compensation packages are higher and billing rates are higher; but, if you want a balance in your life, to be active in your profession, civic activities, community activities, and want to make sure you are not missing your children's plays and sporting events, then smaller firms are better (fewer than 200 lawyers).

Josh Banerje, JD, University of Chicago, sees it like this:

I'm not sure that BigLaw "works" for anyone. I think it's a system that you have to learn and make the most of, and ultimately take a step back every so often and evaluate whether it's still a good fit. In many ways I think BigLaw can be a great training ground for young attorneys because of the sophisticated clients, complex legal issues, firm resources (libraries, research librarians, administrative/staff support), formal training programs, and fellow attorneys who are willing to spend time training new associates. I'm not sure I'd be the attorney I am today if it wasn't for all of the above. I've been in the practice for a while now, and am currently in a secondment position with a big client of the firm, and I have found that I am just as capable of doing the work and advising the client as my colleagues who have been in the practice much longer. That isn't always the case, and here's my take on why.

BigLaw is certainly a sink or swim situation. A young associate must be proactive in almost every way—making sure you're visible to partners, seeking out interesting work, finding partners and associates who are good to work with, and developing mentoring relationships with more experienced attorneys. A great deal of work that is handed to junior associates is high-risk, low-reward; meaning, if you screw up, you will certainly hear about it. On the flip side, if you do a stellar job, you probably won't get a pat on the back . . . perhaps for good reason. For example, no one will congratulate an associate for reviewing thousands of documents efficiently for a document production, finding the case-law that is on point, or getting signature pages out to the client before the overnight FedEx deadline. But an associate will certainly get an earful if he or she is a slow worker, fails to catch typos on deal documents, forgot to attach a document to an e-mail, or sprinted three city blocks through downtown traffic chasing a FedEx truck but ultimately was unsuccessful because Steve Maddens and a pant-suit just aren't quite as good for running as Nikes and Lululemon tights.

To a great extent, BigLaw is what you make of it. Personally, I expect the worst—late nights; weekends; thankless, mindless work; cancelling dinner plans and vacations. It's infuriating when it happens, but it doesn't happen all the time, and when it doesn't, you've manipulated yourself into thinking that it isn't so bad. And a lot of times, it really isn't so bad. I think the key is to know what's important to you and regularly assess how that is changing and whether you are still getting out of BigLaw what you envision you should be. The biggest mistake I see is people not taking a step back to assess their current situation—something I think young associates should do at least annually, if not more frequently. You have to ask yourself the following:

Am I still learning a lot? Am I handling interesting matters and issues that are consistent with my experience level? Am I getting opportunities to work with the partners/associates I want to work with? Am I having (at least some) fun? Am I getting enough sleep? Am I getting to hang out with my significant other, friends, and family? Do I have a hobby? Do I get assignments and immediately think, "crap, I should get a lawyer to do this"?

It seems very basic, but a lot of lawyers are miserable because they let themselves be that way. The bottom line is that BigLaw isn't for everyone, and even if it is good for you now, it might not be later. Anyone considering BigLaw should not be blind to the fact that it is a demanding career choice that involves a lot of sacrifices. And it is increasingly the case that firms are moving away from elevating attorneys to equity partner.

Chris Kratovil, a partner at K&L Gates in Dallas, Texas, says BigLaw is right for the right person. "Many people choose the private sector for (the) wrong reason, such as a liberal arts undergrad who didn't really want to go to law school in the first place but couldn't find anything better to do with life." Chris really wanted to be there and had a prestigious clerkship, his pick of firms, and carefully selected the big firm he chose, making a calculated and informed decision. "You can be happy in firm life," says Chris.

As you may have guessed, the often-cited negative aspect of BigLaw is the low level of career satisfaction. "Nationally, eight out of ten lawyers depart from large firms by their fifth year of practice."[93] There are a lot of reasons for this—long hours and demanding expectations for billing hours and bringing in business, not making partner, and changing priorities in personal life among them. One graduate of NYU who worked for a BigLaw firm in NYC for five years says, "it did not allow balance between personal and professional life." "Lawyers are expressing great dissatisfaction in their large firm practices. The American Bar Foundation's After the JD study of 5,000 associates from the year 2000 on found that 59 percent of the graduates of the top law schools working for large law firms planned to leave within two and a half years."[94] If more law students who went to BigLaw prepared to be there for only five years, it would

---

[93] Nancy Levit and Douglas O. Linder, *The Happy Lawyer: Making a Good Life in the Law* (New York; Oxford University Press, 2010), 226.

[94] www.lawyersatisfactionblog.com/2009/11/will-college-students-continue.html.

change the amount many would be willing to take out in loans to get there.

Some younger law school applicants hear about the job demands and think, "no problem, I can work hard for a few years." Often, however, these are people who never held a full-time, year-round desk job. It's very different from having a boring summer job or a job that is one of many activities in your life. A theme that came through clearly in my research for this book is that the easiest way to ensure your satisfaction with your job is to feel like your days have a purpose. "On average, those in government and public interest work are more satisfied with their work than those in private practice."[95]

In an interview with Nancy Levit and Doug Linder, Doug said: "We were struck by how many of the people we interviewed expressed some unhappiness when their work was just all about the money or they were looking at boring documents in a warehouse that they didn't care one way or the other about. You find a greater level of happiness when you are doing something you care about."

Levit said that the least happy attorneys are those in BigLaw. "Lawyers are voting with their feet by their attrition rates. I enjoyed my time at a big firm. There were complex puzzles to solve, impact litigation, and the resources to do cases right. But a large firm is not right for everyone. Most importantly, students shouldn't be thinking 'Big or Bust.' It's not the brass ring."

The Happy Lawyer offers another explanation—a "lawyer personality" that affects career satisfaction.[96] It argues that highly driven people are not necessarily incredibly happy

---

[95] Levit and Linder, *The Happy Lawyer*, 134.

[96] Career satisfaction is not just a BigLaw issue. According to our survey, [29] percent of attorneys feel overworked and 39 percent report that they are under a great deal of stress.

people, but the quality of being conscientious may help make them better lawyers. It even cites surveys showing that pessimists slightly outperformed their more optimistic peers in law school. "The interplay of attorneys' personality traits and the professional demands of the job can prove toxic."[97] Of course, it can be assumed that (in general) the most highly driven lawyers attended the most competitive law schools and took jobs in the most prestigious firms. Therefore, this group has an especially high tendency to feel dissatisfied with their career choices. The rat race never ends for them until they choose to end it themselves (and get over the pride in their jobs and paychecks) or it is ended for them, usually in a blunt and shocking way during a layoff or by being passed up for a shot at becoming an equity partner.

> I practiced in a large law firm for a few years when I first got out of law school back in the early/mid-1990s. I hated it and left after a few years for the following two reasons:
>
> 1. The pressures for billable hours were just ridiculous, and there was no value placed on expanding your expertise for the customers if it wasn't billable. For example, I [was assigned to] research and write one of the partner's papers and presentation for an upcoming seminar (which was pushed to this kind of deadline because he wouldn't let me work on it due to preference for billable work first and I finally said that we would miss the deadline if I couldn't focus on **his** presentation).

---

[97] Levit and Linder, *The Happy Lawyer*, 76.

I worked from about 7 a.m. to 11 p.m. every day for about 3 or 4 days. After I was finished, he said "I expect you to make up for those hours in billable work now." REALLY?! Make up 64 hours in the context of 10- to 12-hour days as it is?!

2. I brought in a very large client—one that one of the partners in my group had tried to land herself and failed. I had the relationship with a key person in that client's company, but when we signed them up as a client I had to fight to be the attorney in charge of the account. They put her as the "partner in charge," but technically I was supposed to be the attorney in charge of the day-to-day work. She refused to involve me in anything she did and tried to take over all of the work for them. This was the inherent competition for the labels of partner in charge and responsible attorney that happens all the time inside the law firm.

I went in-house after leaving the law firm in the mid-/late-1990s and have never left that practice. I now have my own business providing part-time/interim chief legal officers for companies that aren't in a position to hire a full-time employee to perform that role.

—Dawn E. Ely, Esq., President & Founder,
Palladium Chief Legal Officers,
Atlanta, GA

Managing a Life in BigLaw

We spoke to a BigLaw senior associate in San Francisco who really enjoys his work, especially now that he has learned how to balance time in the office with time away from the office.

Managing your work and your life is the hardest part of life as a lawyer. Early on, you have to earn the trust of your colleagues by working hard, delivering quality work, making good decisions, being accountable, and being flexible. Once you've started to earn that trust, you have to slowly train your partners and clients to respect your time and your life outside the firm. If you're in the middle of doing something fun on a Saturday night, let the call go to voicemail, and write an e-mail back when you get a chance. If you get an e-mail at 4 a.m. that isn't really that urgent, respond when you wake up at 7:30 or 8, indicate that you are handling it, and will follow up as soon as you are able. Sometimes you just have to act like you are busier than you actually are. Partners'/clients' perception that you are very busy (but not impossible to get a hold of) is a good thing. Work from home one day if you need a break from the typical grind, or call in sick if you really *really* need a day to unscramble— food poisoning is a good one, because it can happen to anyone, is usually quite debilitating, doesn't make you seem weak or like a hypochondriac, and you can "recover" in a day (of course, you can't do this frequently, and you certainly don't want to get caught out at a bar taking shots—if you're on Facebook, beware of "check-ins" and people tagging you in pictures). You will, of course, get flak from time to time, but you always apologize for responding late, be sincere about it, and move on with your day.

This associate provides a great example of how your ability to keep things in perspective can help predict whether your personality is a good fit for BigLaw. But, if you don't think you'll be happy going to BigLaw, then don't go. Professor Thane Rosenbaum wrote a scathing book about the legal profession, and claims his years as a young BigLaw lawyer were tainted by discontent and boredom. However, it seems many of his complaints about practicing law from the top of a skyscraper, far removed from real people and their problems, would be nullified if he worked as most lawyers work: with people. Whether family law, estate planning, criminal law, or personal injury law, there is a way to help real people solve their problems. When I told my husband (a worker's compensation lawyer) about Rosenbaum's complaints that all he did was write memos, my husband reminded me that two days after passing the bar he was in court arguing a motion. If you want action immediately, don't go to BigLaw. When I was a summer associate, I went to court and was accompanied by a partner and a seven-year associate. Why on earth couldn't the seven-year associate handle the simple motion hearing? Why did the client want to pay for three of us to go to court?

> *If you are going to a top law school and taking out loans just so you can go to BigLaw, think about taking a scholarship to another school, graduating with minimal debt, and having the freedom to take a job that allows you to work with people and go to court (or whatever else you decide is important to you). You may be much happier in the long run. And I'm not the only person who feels this way.*

I don't agree that you necessarily always go to Harvard over a fourth tier school. There are a lot of reasons not to go to the best school you get into—the biggest thing to look to is the students who go to school there and how much are they like the kind of people you would like to be. Too many students go to the top 5 schools instead of a top 25, and you can get just as good an education at any of these, all with faculty graduating from the same schools. They choose the higher school to validate themselves, to look good to other people. It's hard to convince them otherwise; they can't have regrets. I would hope they understand that there are more important things— where they go will shape them, but they need to visit and make a choice about where they will be satisfied with their choice. There are several reasons I think people out of the top law schools aren't particularly happy: downward comparison—people coming out of fourth tier law schools are just happy to be lawyers,[98] often first-generation lawyers, and it's a position that provides status, etc. For people coming out of top law schools, they compare themselves with their undergraduate friends who are CEOs, politicians, making movies, and their lives don't seem particularly exciting. Also, a sense of high expectations/entitlement comes with people who have always been successful in everything they've done.

—Douglas O. Linder, co-author of *The Happy*

---

[98] Levit and Linder, *The Happy Lawyer*, 231. "It is also worth noting that there is an inverse correlation between happiness in the profession and the ranking of the law school attended. Lawyers are somewhat more likely to be happy with their careers if they went to a fourth tier law school as opposed to a top law school."

Lawyer and a Professor of Law at the University of
Missouri-Kansas City (graduate of Stanford)

It's important to keep in mind that BigLaw is not the only
way to practice law; in fact, only a small percentage of lawyers
are employed by large firms. "[B]ig firms employing fewer than
15 percent of the nation's 1 million attorneys are important, but
they're not the only game in town. In fact, employment in those
firms probably shouldn't even be a goal for most students."[99]

Our interviews with lawyers garnered some interesting
perspectives on BigLaw:

- One attorney who has been practicing law for 6 to 10
  years said, "My experience is with BigLaw only. But
  based on that, I think law is a terrible career choice if
  you have any desire for so-called work–life balance.
  It simply does not exist. The financial incentive just
  isn't strong enough to make up for the endless stress
  and degradation. I'd advise people to go into finance
  instead."

- One of our survey respondents who attended the
  University of Chicago said she "left a very large
  national firm for a smaller, regional firm with better
  hours and job security, but lower pay."

- One attorney left private practice to work for the
  government because there was "not enough upward
  mobility [and the] type of work provided was more
  like paralegal work. All the meaningful work went to
  partners."

- Another attorney, who went on to become Senior

---

[99] Steven J. Harper article in *Circuit Rider*; www.7thcircuitbar.org/associations/1507/
files/Circuit%20Rider%20Vol%2010.pdf.

Director of Business and Legal Affairs for a major entertainment company, reflects on her days in private practice by saying "I had zero personal life."

The important thing is to be honest with yourself about what you're willing to put up with and how important the money is to you. Even if you do decide that BigLaw is the right place for you, you'll face a lot of competition. Scott Carter says, "I am increasingly hearing about BigLaw introducing new permanent associate non-partner track positions, thus making traditional, partner track associate positions even more competitive." Deborah Epstein Henry also sees this trend as a consultant for large law firms. She says new staff level positions within the upward trajectory to partnership, at lower pay levels, are being introduced; she worries that the traditional pipeline of talented lawyers (who then go on to run the BigLaw firms, become in-house counsel for big companies, etc.) will dry up if law firms go this route. "In-house legal departments have historically plucked well-trained law firm talent to be the future leaders of the in-house community, and they may no longer have the same opportunities to do so. Also, new model law firms—including virtual firms and firms founded on alternative fee and secondment models—will no longer have the same ability to hire trained talent to perform in their environments."[100]

---

[100] "Combatting Junior Lawyer Fallout: Part I," http://lawandreorder.com/press/press21.pdf.

CHAPTER 11

SOLO PRACTICE:
HAVING THE BEST
(OR WORST) BOSS EVER

THE attorneys who report the highest levels of job satisfaction are those who work for themselves. I identify with them. When I worked in law firms, "face time" (being the one in the office first to make the coffee and the last to turn the lights out) was a matter of pride. The money felt good, working to solve clients' problems was interesting and challenging, talking about legal issues and trial strategy invigorated me. On the down side, it was a lot of hours, a lot of stress, no time for lunch or errands, and if I was in a deposition when it was time to pick up my daughter, I had to make some pretty speedy arrangements. However, owning my own business has improved my quality of life in every way. A lot of lawyers feel the same way. We put out a request on HARO asking for responses from lawyers who left bigger law firms to start their own practices and heard some really inspiring stories. I am sharing a lot of examples and perspectives here because the positive response was so overwhelming, and it's something that I believe not enough pre-law and law students think about while they are in law school. Keeping in mind your likely career trajectory (the step you take after your first or second job out of law school) will help you make wise decisions about whether and where to attend law school and how to spend your time during law school.

- Erin Giglia graduated from University of San Diego School of Law in 2001. She finished in the top 10 percent of her class and was a member of the *San Diego Law Review*. After law school, she practiced at Brobeck, Phleger & Harrison, and then at Snell & Wilmer. In 2009, she transitioned out of traditional legal practice by starting Montage Legal Group.

    It is not a law firm, it is a network of free-lance attorneys. All of our attorneys opted out of BigLaw in favor of career flexibility, and now do freelance projects for lawyers and law firms (in addition to other pursuits). Montage now has 20 attorneys in our network, from schools like Harvard and Stanford and trained at firms like Latham & Watkins and Gibson, Dunn & Crutcher. Each attorney is indepen-dent. Montage joins its attorneys together by providing support, marketing, networking, billing, collections, and other administrative support. Think of a small firm that is busy but not busy enough to hire a full-time associate. That firm can bring in a temporary attorney trained at a big firm who gets a low hourly rate. Even if the firm upcharges the rate to their client, the rate is still much lower than an associate's hourly rate, and the law firm gets to keep the profit with zero hiring risk.[101]

- Cindy Salvo says BigLaw is all-consuming.

    I started my career in BigLaw NYC and the hours were horrendous. We were expected to work until at least 10 in the evening, and every other weekend. The pressure was enormous. I left BigLaw NYC to go to BigLaw New Jersey. It was much better there. I worked a lot fewer hours (much less pay!), and I was still considered one of the highest-billing attorneys in the litigation group. After a number of years at BigLaw New Jersey, I decided to start my own practice. I did so for many reasons, not the least of which is that I wanted to be my own boss. I started my own practice in 2006. I put in a lot of hours just trying to build the business, but at least my long hours were for myself. Now I am doing extremely well. I continue to do commercial litigation, and am very busy. I have other attorneys working for me. We have also expanded into the divorce/family law area. I am making far more money now than I ever made in BigLaw, and working very hard, but I *love* the freedom, the autonomy, and the excitement. I occasionally take a contingency fee

---

[101] The firm also addresses an issue that is discussed in Chapter 14: What to do with all of the women lawyers who decide to take time off from practice to raise children. Montage offers a way to re-enter the work force or work part time in a world that operates mostly on billable hours.

matter that sometimes brings in big bucks—I couldn't do that while I was working at BigLaw! In short, starting my own firm was definitely the right answer for me.

- Although Kevin Houchin says it's not always easy to be a solo practitioner, he is "generally happy and way better off in my current situation than I would be as a staff lawyer in a firm. At least I have the freedom and power to make changes to correct course as I go along."

- Melissa Herman (Herman & Russo, PC, in Woodstock, Georgia), shared her reasons for opening her own law firm.

  Life at the big bankruptcy law firm began with a 1.5 to 2 hour commute each morning. There was no flexibility in the times in which I worked. I had to be there at 8:30 and I had to stay until the last client was seen. Unlike most large law firms, my former firm operated on a flat-fee basis and did not do billable hours. It survives off of volume—appointments are set every 15 minutes and are usually triple-booked. Attorneys are discouraged from spending more than 15 minutes with clients and lunches were verboten. This makes for angry, hostile clients. Support staff retention was always poor, and the firm did not go out of its way to hire stellar support staff. I handled about 100 hearings per week and I always felt I was unprepared. I usually got home around 7:30 each night. The firm was open on Saturdays, and there was a lot of pressure to go in on Saturdays. I truly dreaded going to work on Mondays. The positives were: the pay was ok, and there were benefits that included health insurance, I had three weeks of vacation time, I had the major holidays off, and I was eligible for a large car allowance ($750). I also received $250 a month for gas, and I did not have to do any marketing or rainmaking and I did not have any overhead.

The positives were not enough to outweigh the negatives. I practiced on my own in Louisiana prior to moving to Georgia and decided it might be time to go out on my own. My husband and I decided to open our own bankruptcy firm. The positives and negatives have almost switched. I have a short and pleasant commute, great support staff, great clients who usually pay, and I now have the time to be prepared for court. The negatives are long hours, high health insurance costs; it is hard to take vacations, and we now have stresses associated with owning a business such as generating business. Overall, the positives outweigh the negatives, and I am much happier now than I was.

- Gary Massey Jr. of Chattanooga, Tennessee, says:

    I left a large corporate law firm to open my own law practice with a partner in December 2000. I graduated in the top 3 percent of my class in law school and served as an editor on the law review. I had clerked for the large firm after my second year in law school and they offered me a job, which I happily took. At first, I was so proud to be working in a tall building with dozens of high-powered lawyers handling big cases. While working there, I became disillusioned that one of the most important issues in my life was how many hours I had billed that month. Such thoughts occupied a considerable part of my conscious brain. Not only was I disillusioned, but I also started feeling guilty that I was representing the wrong clients. I defended one case in particular where the lawyer for the injured employee simply did not know what he was doing. We took advantage of that by simply offering a little bit of money early in the case to settle it and the lawyer told his client to take it. I still feel guilty when I think of what that lady should have received versus what we paid her.

    Not long after that, I went to a party our law firm threw for a bunch of insurance adjuster clients. I was involved in a conversation at this party where the adjusters were bragging and laughing about the injured claimants whose cases they had settled for pennies on the dollar. I left that party knowing I had to switch sides—I couldn't work for these people anymore. That's when a fellow associate and I struck out on our own.

My former partner has now left our firm, but I'm representing people who have been injured and feel great about the service I provide to the world. Many of my clients come to me after another lawyer has messed up their case which makes it more difficult to help them, but I have a special sympathy for people in this position. I now have about five lawyers, counting those who work with me 'of counsel' (which means most of them also have legal services they perform separate from my firm).

• Andrew Flusche graduated from the University of Virginia and began working for a nonprofit. When budget cuts came eight months later, he was laid off. After that experience, I decided I never wanted to have a boss again. I didn't even look for another employee position; I immediately hung out my shingle." Andrew started by working out of his house. "You really don't need much to practice law: a license, malpractice insurance, a phone, and a computer. I now have a traditional office and an assistant, but it took two years to build up to that." Although he endured a different kind of stress than most recent law school graduates, he is very happy with his decision. "I love my autonomy. I'm the captain of my ship. I've been blessed so far to have a growing practice, but even if things start to slow down, I'll still be in charge and can work to turn it around." He also credits his lifestyle as one of the benefits of self-employment. "I work a lot—70 hours is a normal week for me. That's not all client activity; a lot of it is managing the practice, marketing, etc. But since I'm the boss, I'm able to choose when and how I work. My office is 1.1 miles from my house. I come home for lunch with my wife most days. And I can easily work from home when I want to."

For law students considering starting their own practice after graduation, Andrew offers the following advice: "If you know where you want to practice, start networking early. You can join lots of bar associations at a very low student rate. Start developing mentor relationships during law school with folks in your geographic area and people who have practices like you hope to have. It's never too early to start making friends. Those friends are a HUGE key to making it as a solo."

This was a common theme among the advice offered by solo practitioners. "What you know is only half the battle. Who you know is incredibly important. Networking can lead to a new job, a new client, or other opportunities. People don't hire lawyers from a phone book or a website. They ask around. You want your name to come up when someone is looking for a lawyer in your practice area," says Bret Stone.

Another theme that emerged is having the flexibility to

pursue other interests. One person who responded to our survey is a solo practitioner who also serves as mayor of his small town. "I probably bill about 1,500 hours a year and spend more than 1,000 hours serving the community in elected office. The first pays far more than the second but I enjoy the second far more than the first." Being a solo practitioner is what allows him to take on work as a public servant.

For those of you intrigued by the idea of working for yourself at some point in your law career, I highly recommend reading Spencer Marc Aronfeld's *Make It Your Own Law Firm: The Ultimate Law Student's Guide to Owning, Managing, and Marketing Your Own Successful Law Firm* (Bloomington, IN: AuthorHouse, 2011). It provides an honest account of what it's like to start your own law firm right out of law school, the importance of keeping costs down, and of maximizing networking opportunities. It should be a must-read for all law students.[102]

---

[102] To listen to my Blog Talk Radio interview with him on this topic, go to www.blogtalkradio.com/ann-levine/2011/06/30/prepare-for-law-school-and-your-legal-career-now.

CHAPTER 12

GOING CORPORATE OR IN-HOUSE

MANY lawyers leave big firms to work for the firm's clients as general counsel. This provides a steady paycheck, more predictable hours, and allows the attorneys to become a bigger part of the solution rather than coming into the decision-making process only after a mistake has been made or a problem has presented itself. Dawn Ely was kind enough to provide such extensive advice on this topic that she essentially wrote the chapter for me. The following sections are Dawn's personal comments taken from interviews and material she supplied. Dawn is President of Palladium Chief Legal Officers in Atlanta, Georgia. After graduating from Mercer Law in 1993, she worked for a large law firm and then went in-house.

The Difference between Corporate Practice and Being In-House Counsel

One of the many reasons why I find being in-house so much more satisfying is because you are more involved with the business—you are *in* the business, having an impact in daily operations and preventing problems and helping to steer the ship before it hits a glacier. Law firm practice relegates you to acting when a client calls you—which is reactive and puts you in a position mostly of fixing a problem or just giving theory and rule analyses that result in research and writing a memo in most cases. Some people like that role, I'm just not one of them. My personality is one that is more comfortable with finding solutions and possibilities, not just identifying problems and putting forth an analysis of why they are problems.

The difference between being an in-house lawyer and a law firm lawyer is not just the difference in the activities performed and skill sets, but it's a difference in the mindset. Usually, people are better suited for one role or the other, but rarely both or either (although there are some who do both well). Those who have crossed over from law firm to in-house have found it takes several months to get used to the difference in the practice, and some never acclimate well and remain a "fish out of water" in the corporate environment. For example, in a management team meeting, if the other business managers talk about taking a course of action that presents some legal risk unseen to them (and I've never been in a management team meeting where that was not the case), the law firm lawyer's mentality and response is usually "you can't do that because it violates XYZ law or could present ABC risk," whereas the experienced in-house lawyer's mentality and response is "we really shouldn't do that because of XYZ or ABC, but we can do JKL instead and it minimizes the chances of XYZ or ABC occurring, and I think JKL is the least business-restrictive alternative to minimizing these risks." If an in-house lawyer tells a CEO that he or she can't do something without telling them what they *can* do instead, they have little value to the business and will be out of a job in short order. In order to tell the CEO what he or she *can* do, the lawyer has to know the business operations and objectives well enough to be able to make that suggestion. A remote law firm lawyer will never be in a position to do that because that takes knowledge of day-to-day operations to be able to make that suggestion, which they will never have. I've seen many misplaced lawyers who were in in-house positions, but with law firm mentalities who would respond, "I don't know what you should do—that's a business decision. Make another choice in your actions based on the rules I'm telling you about, and come back with a different plan and we can talk again." These misplaced lawyers mistakenly believe there is a distinction between business and legal issues and don't want to participate in the business operations or decisions—they still have the "ivory tower" mentality and provide little value to the business because they are effectively operating as law firm lawyers who aren't part of the business, and the business already has law firm lawyers they can call on for this type of advice. These attorneys are rarely successful inside business environments and are often "downsized" at the first opportunity.

Although it is true that there are decisions that are more appropriate for legal personnel versus business operational managers to make about the issues, the issues themselves are like double-sided coins with business impact on one side and legal impact on the other. There is virtually no decision to be made or activity to engage in by the business managers that doesn't also have a legal-oriented implication—some are easy, some not so much. In the vast majority of cases, the business operational managers don't see those legal sides of their decisions and actions, and that's what the in-house counsel is there for—to walk hand-in-hand with the business operational managers to help them accomplish the business goals with the least risk or at the risk tolerance level of the CEO. A very large component of the responsibility of the in-house counsel is risk assessment—both in terms of severity and likelihood. An example I give often is the fact that we all face the risk that we could walk outside, cross the street, and get hit by a bus pulling out of nowhere. The severity is pretty high, but the likelihood is pretty low, so we don't manage our lives by that and not venture outside. Instead, we take minimal precautions of looking both ways as we cross streets, and we've done a minimal and nonrestrictive act to minimize even further that low likelihood. This is the same for legal and business risks. Most law firm lawyers are entirely risk averse and are uncomfortable making risk assessments and taking any risk. Although we have plenty of laws in this country, there is rarely a definitive roadmap for how any law would be applied in various circumstances. For example, a company maintains a dual channel of distribution of their products—both a direct sales force and an indirect using distributors/original equipment manufacturers, etc., to which the company is not only a supplier but also then a competitor competing with them in their direct sales activities. This could present antitrust concerns if the competitors share pricing. So, where does the knowledge of pricing for the indirect channel and the direct channel become appropriate? At the CEO level only, or can it go down to the VP level or the national or regional manager level? There are no organizational charts in these laws, so we have to make our best judgment based on our knowledge of the law and our risk assessment of the burden to the business versus the likelihood of us making a wrong decision on where that level should be and the resulting legal penalty. In this particular case, I engaged an outside law firm antitrust expert to help guide me and validate my thoughts to be sure I had a second legal opinion in this highly specialized area of the law.

So, there is most definitely a role for both law firm and in-house lawyers—they just perform different roles (not unlike the CFO of a company versus the company's CPA firm). The in-house has to be knowledgeable enough in many areas of the law to at least identify an issue whereas most law firm lawyers have a particular specialty, and they develop that to the greatest extent. So, as I say frequently, the in-house counsel are a mile wide and an inch deep (with the exception of their industry expertise areas, such as health care, technology, etc., in which their companies operate) and the law firm lawyers are an inch wide and a mile deep in their specialties. The in-house counsel deal with 80 percent of the day-to-day issues and identify the need for the specialists in the areas and issues that go beyond that 80 percent of their knowledge base. So, both types of lawyers and practices are needed, but they are very different from one another and require different skill sets and personality/mind sets. Law school students should be exposed to both types of practices to see where their preferences fall. However, below are categories with examples of questions that they should ask themselves to see if they want to explore either or both.

Hours to Be Worked

Law Firm—extreme pressure from partners to have a minimum number of billable hours, which usually translates into working 15 to 25 percent more hours than what you can actually bill for. So, if you're required to bill 1,820 hours/year (a common minimum), that means 35 hours/week are billable. Because you have administrative duties—getting up to speed on topics and issues to be that expert, you have a continuing legal education question, partner's continuing legal education presentations you have to do, lunch, breaks, administrative firm meetings, and many other activities that can't be billed to the client, that means that you'll end up working a minimum of 45 hours/week of actual work—not including time taken for lunches, etc., and even more for those weeks where you have more than an hour a day of non-billable time—which will be a lot of weeks. For those people who are highly efficient, they can suffer because they won't have the hours if they get things done well quicker unless there is a pile of work just waiting each time you are finished. This doesn't always happen for associates and sometimes associates have to seek out work from partners—especially to keep up their billable hours.

In-House—pressure is not on how many hours you work, but on getting work done for the business in a timely manner so as not to hold up sales and business activities. This ends up translating into often times as many hours as you work in the law firm, but it is more under your own control with a pressure for timeliness versus just hours. This practice encourages and rewards efficiency versus time taken.

Interaction with the Clients

Law Firm—as you're starting out, you have limited and very sporadic interaction with the client. It will usually be by phone as you're participating with higher level lawyers or maybe an occasional face-to-face meeting. As you get more years in practice, it will be more often, but will still always be sporadic and mostly by phone. In most cases, unless you're actively working on a project, it will be mostly when the client calls you with some issue. For introverted personalities, this is usually preferable.

In-house—every second of every day is client interaction. You are part of the client. Often the reason that in-house work long hours is because during the day their door is revolving as business managers come in and out and they are involved in business meetings, etc. The only time an in-house can often get their "own" work done of contract drafting and review, etc., is before 8 a.m. or after 5 p.m. when the rest of the business leaves. For those who have a strong business mind or inclination and who like to be where business decisions are made and impromptu discussions and advice are a daily part of the job, this environment would be preferable.

Type of Work Done

Law Firm—project-based work is the norm here—whether it is working on due diligence for a mergers and acquisitions deal, researching a particular issue and writing a memo, drafting a complex legal agreement, preparing for a hearing or a trial, etc. There will be usually little known about the business other than what information is given to you by the partner. You may be given an opportunity to ask the client questions by phone. From time to time, you will get a client calling with an urgent situation or question that they need to know quickly, but that is rare. Time spent getting up to speed on reading substantive articles will usually have to be spent on off-hours because there isn't time during the work day to spend more than about 15 minutes on such things. Again, introverted and/or conceptual or academic personalities will likely prefer this environment. This environment thrives on theory and rule-based thinking.

In-house—no day goes by the way you plan it. Most days are "on the fly" and interrupted with things that come up—whether it's a customer issue, a strategic alliance issue, a personnel issue, a crazy/nasty/threatening letter from a regulatory authority or competitor, etc. There is a lot of verbal advisory work done without a lot of time for researching an issue before the business will act one way or the other. The written legal work can range from writing a company policy to drafting personnel employment/separation agreements to office leases and operational documents such as customer contracts and strategic alliance documents. Those students who are not comfortable or confident to trust their statements without significant research behind it, or who are completely risk averse and aren't comfortable in giving any kind of risk assessment, will not feel comfortable or do well in this environment.

Pay and Future Advancement

Law Firm—most everyone is aware of the "partner track" for the law firm. You work your butt off for six to eight years, and if you've had enough billable hours and are deemed to be sufficient in recruiting new clients, you will make the partner level where you can earn significant sums that would include a percentage of your own billings. The more you work, the more you earn.

In-house—the salary- and bonus-based earning capacity is not usually what it is in the law firm unless you get to the level of a General Counsel for a Fortune 1,000 or Fortune 500 company. Few attain this level. However, depending on the type of company you go to and the size of the legal department, there are more opportunities for advancement to a higher level than in the law firm in the early years of a career. There is still some competition with law firms in hiring lawyers, so companies are not ridiculously far behind the law firm salaries (unlike the government). Once you hit about years 7 to 10 in your career, you are at the divisional or general counsel level and the opportunities for moving up or earning more will usually come from moving from company to company. However, stock options for this type of position are common and can be quite lucrative and could easily equal or surpass in value the salary/bonus-earning capability in the law firm.

> Mona Stone, former in-house counsel and now an attorney with a major law firm, says, "The old mentality is that [in-house] work isn't as glamorous or high paying, but this is changing and hours are heavier and the job is more stressful. The corporate lifestyle is not as forgiving anymore, and you must be able to handle a matter start to finish instead of calling outside lawyers whenever a problem arises."
>
> Another interesting aspect to practicing law as an in-house lawyer is that it's not necessarily difficult to transfer between industries. I have a friend who has served in this capacity for a health care giant, then in the gaming industry, and now in the entertainment field. With each move, he climbed up the ladder despite not having industry-specific experience.

CHAPTER 13

LITIGATOR OR DEAL MAKER?

LAWYERS generally fall into one of these two categories. You probably know which category works best for you before you even start law school. Litigation is known as being the fast-paced, think-on-your-feet, television-worthy area of law practice. Litigators are the fighters: instead of drafting contracts, they argue the boundaries of the contracts. This practice includes court time, yes, but also client time, research time, motion writing, and engaging in the evidentiary process (including the less than glamorous process of civil discovery). Corporate or transactional law, on the other hand, is more proactive. "In general, a corporate transactional attorney needs to be a problem solver and a part of the team working on a business transaction (e.g., deal). A litigator's job is generally to fight first and settle later," says Joshua Rabinowitz, who earned his JD and an LLM in Taxation from the University of San Diego. He observes the difference between what he does and what his partners who are litigators do:

In general, transactional attorneys' hours tend to be a more steady pattern, with longer hours worked when closing business transactions (e.g., deals). A litigator tends to have more extreme swings in hours, depending on the stage of each of his or her cases (e.g., right before and during trial a litigator's lifestyle tends to be miserable). Also, litigators tend to deal with clients and others who are experiencing a lot of stress and problems. Transactional attorneys tend to deal with clients and others who are all working toward a common goal—completing a business transaction.

Mona Stone adds, "People who do corporate law don't have to go to court—it's more of a desk job and interacting with clients. It can be very time-sensitive and cyclical. When a deal hits, as a contract lawyer, you're pulling all-nighters with high stakes and high-level work within a very concentrated period of time." Once you decide whether you're best suited to be a litigator or a deal maker, you then have innumerable practice areas to consider. Brandon Scheele makes that point that not all litigators are trial attorneys.

I feel that people misperceive this all the time, especially as a law student. "Do you want to litigate or not litigate" is not the question. You could be in business litigation or construction litigation and you're not a trial lawyer. If you're a litigator in some specialties, you're a transactional lawyer. It encompasses so many different kinds of law practice. I think it's a poor category. If you're a bankruptcy lawyer you're a litigator, but you're not going to jury trial; you have a hearing in front of the judge, but you're not taking depositions. The practice is 100 percent different from the personal injury lawyer who is taking 5 to 10 depositions per week, jury trials several times a year, and is fully immersed in the jury system. What does it mean to be a trial attorney? It's an awesome job if you want to have a high-volume, high-intensity, high-energy practice. The calendar is full every day: you have 5, 6, 10 cases you're working on every day. I'll touch as many as 20 different cases in a day. I have 1.5 days in my office out of every week. The rest of the time I'm taking depositions, at hearings, doing site inspections. My calendar is completely full. I'm always on the go. I get 100 e-mails a day and 25 phone calls a day.

If you try one or more areas of law, as suggested previously in Chapter 1, and like it (or don't like it), that doesn't mean you will or won't like other areas of the law because practice areas can be so different from each other. In the following discussion are some examples of the nuances between different areas of law.

Some transactional attorneys practice generally, helping clients with business and personal needs ranging from real estate to tax to setting up corporations, but some are highly specialized. Here are some examples:

- One transportation law attorney who graduated from Georgetown says his job involves monitoring regulatory and legal updates, drafting (e-mails, memos, contracts, federal agency pleadings), and researching regulatory issues. But, he says that even within this narrow field attorneys should pick a particular industry/sub-field on which to focus. "Most transportation attorneys are not generalists; some handle unique personal injury litigation for railroad employees, some represent shippers before federal agencies, some help state and local agencies procure construction projects."

- Mark Rothenberg has represented developers and now works for a utility company. He feels that his work is tangible. "I like seeing the results of my work which typically include shopping centers, houses, offices—places where people live, shop, congregate, work, etc."

- Bret Stone practices in an area that is cited by many law school applicants as an intended area of interest: environmental law. His practice blends litigation and transactional work. "From responding to problems such as a contaminated site to developing and implementing forward-thinking sustainability management systems for both public and private clients, [the job requires] excellent writing, personal communication, and business acumen."

A great example of the many ways of practicing transactional law is entertainment law. A lot of law school applicants say this is what they hope to do with their degrees. Really, it's glorified contract law in one of three forms: (1) working in a law firm on behalf of the studios; (2) representing an individual entering into a contract with the studios; or (3) working for the studios themselves. This area of law is highly competitive, so I spoke with Leon Liu, Vice President and Senior Counsel for HBO and a graduate of Harvard, about how he started his career and what advice he has to offer those who hope to pursue this field.

Leon knew as a 1L that he wanted to be a transactional attorney as opposed to a litigator, and spent his 2L year taking courses related to entertainment law and copyright. For his 2L summer, he accepted a job with a firm that came to interview on campus. The main attraction of the firm was not its name recognition but the fact that it had an entertainment law department. At the end of his summer with the firm, Leon specifically requested a position in that department. "It was competitive and it came down to whether they liked me (and, of course, the school name helped)." Below, Leon shares more about his job responsibilities and dynamics of his employment on each of the three sides of the industry.

Entertainment Law

At a big corporate firm, you usually serve as outside counsel on the transactional side for various entities/companies. You do production work for studios, like if they are shooting a movie sometimes instead of doing production legal work in-house, they'll do a negotiated flat-fee hand-off to an outside firm for the riders, location releases, clearances, permission to use a film clip, etc. Mostly it's contract work, just different types of contracts. We worked on a range of contract issues including music licenses, copyright renewal and termination, e-commerce, sweepstakes advertisements, and promotions.

The variety of tasks was good training. Big firms train you on what to do and the basic law, but entertainment boutique firms don't have time to teach you. After two years at the firm, I got a phone call from my next firm, Armstrong Hirsch, that represents talent—actors, writers, directors, producers—primarily opposite the studios in their deals. They don't take people right out of law school. I wasn't 100 percent keyed into the entertainment industry when I started, and you should be and you need to be if you want to do it. I didn't even know the firm when they called me, and people who knew entertainment law knew that's where I should go but I wasn't involved enough to know that.

At the new firm the legal work was still contracts, but there was much more handholding and more interaction with clients because before the clients were big companies and you'd be dealing with inside counsel or executives. At the talent firm I was dealing with the person, their agent, their manager, and sometimes their business manager. We took commission so it was a different business model entirely. It can be much more lucrative than working at a big law firm, or even being a partner at a big law firm. At a big law firm, you make money by having people work under you. At a boutique firm, it's the opposite. Our commission was a standard 5 percent, so it makes no sense to spend extra time (or have extra people). A lot of the deals are very precedent-based—repeat-player business with contracts where you can use pretty much the same agreement as the last time the person worked for the studio. What makes it interesting is the dollar amounts involved.

I left it all behind to go in-house because part of the talent thing is that it's very competitive and you have to get business [chasing whomever] is the new hottest person. It's a very hard grind. At a big law firm, whether you're litigation or transactional, you're not working on 100 matters at a time but a handful of clients and projects; you don't have on your plate at one time 100 clients and 100 different matters like I did at the talent firm. You have to balance everybody's needs, and it's a lot of pressure to do that. And you have to schmooze and bring in business and build relationships with agents and managers to get referrals. It's a very relationship-based business. After seven and a half years, I moved in-house to a studio. I'd had experience opposite every studio and I knew what everybody else does and I wanted a lifestyle. In-house experience of entertainment attorney is more like what I did at the first law firm, but for one client and much more in depth.

I'm now who I was arguing against when I was a talent attorney. I work on any and all legal matters to do with development and production of programs. There is a distinction between business affairs and legal affairs. Business affairs primarily negotiates and closes deals but doesn't focus on the paper as much; you don't have to be an attorney to do this, but many are. Legal affairs is primarily just the paper—doing contracts and also once the show or movie is being produced, all of the production legal stuff (clearances, releases, etc.). At HBO, I am primarily doing legal not business affairs, but some studios call it "business and legal affairs" where people take care of both.

When hiring an attorney in any of these positions, I look to experience first. A lot of this stuff needs to be learned. Even if you come from a great school, I prefer someone who can hit the ground running. The school is important but not overriding. At a big law firm it's a little different because corporate culture trains people right out of law school, but there isn't a lot of time to train people in other settings. Studios aren't that snobby about schools.

Entertainment law is very competitive. If you don't like your job, there's a line out the door for people wanting [to take your place]. People are attracted by the glamour; this is part of why I was drawn to it. But it's also very competitive and so the likelihood of you getting into this versus something else is less. What's the best way to get into entertainment law? Try to get into an entertainment department of a big law firm and then go from there. It's also kind of about luck and who you know. A lot of the times it's asking if you can do an informational meeting—this is getting much more common as a way to get people to see you and notice you.

—Leon Liu, Vice President and Senior Counsel,
HBO (graduate of Harvard)

Litigation also takes many forms. For every litigator fighting on behalf of companies, there is a litigator fighting on behalf of those who claim to be wronged by companies. Public interest attorneys may be involved in litigation with the government, and the government may be in litigation with the government (as in the case of public defenders and prosecutors). Mona Stone, who practices labor and employment law, is not in court every day but says there are certain things you have to be comfortable with to be a litigator of any kind. "You have to be able to think quickly and handle high pressure from opposing counsel and judge. You have to have thick skin." Below are some examples of careers in litigation.

Personal Injury

Some litigators do jury trials and others do only court hearings or write appeals. Perhaps the most recognizable (as in, most often played on TV) litigators are plaintiff's attorneys, sardonically referred to as "ambulance chasers." These attorneys represent the "little guy" against "the man" in personal injury and other torts, workers compensation, medical malpractice, employment discrimination, and civil rights claims.

As mentioned in Chapter 8, plaintiff attorneys are usually paid by contingency fees. Therefore, the income is less predictable, but of course they have higher potential for windfalls (to make up for the losses). It requires you to be a little more hungry for work. "Being a personal injury lawyer requires the most diverse skill set of any area of the law," according to Spencer Aronfeld,[103] author and a board certified attorney in civil trial by the Florida Bar. "One has to have the ability to care about another, the guts to fight on their behalf regardless of the strength of the foe, a thick skin, the study skills of a Talmudic scholar, acting skills, and the steely nerves of a high stakes poker player. I know of no other area of the law that requires so many different skill sets to succeed." Of course, in addition to these skills, personal injury attorneys are usually also worrying about running a business. In Aronfeld's opinion, "No area of the law has the highest potential for financial success and ruin. It is no surprise that many of the great personal injury trial lawyers of my generation are behind bars, bankrupt, or both, because—if the balance of skills becomes unbalanced—it is a recipe for disaster."

---

[103] Spencer Marc Aronfeld, *Make It Your Own Law Firm: The Ultimate Law Student's Guide to Owning, Managing, and Marketing Your Own Successful Law Firm* (Bloomington, IN: Author house, 2011).

Public Interest

Kevin Probst, an Equal Justice Works Fellow, agrees that a day in his life is fast-paced, exciting, challenging, and at times, exhausting.

> If I'm not on intake in the main office, I'm likely meeting with several clients in a given day—in addition to working on my cases, of course. Examples include disability and other Social Security cases, public benefits, unemployment compensation, consumer law, special education and tax, to name just a few. As an Equal Justice Works Fellow directing a medical-legal partnership for children, I'm on-site with my medical partner one day each week, conducting new client intakes and meeting with current clients. Through my project, I also handle quite a few eviction and other landlord-tenant cases. In sum, my daily duties often include researching the law, drafting pleadings, investigating and developing the facts in my cases, meeting with clients, negotiating with opposing counsel, representing clients in administrative hearings, and delivering community education presentations.

Kevin's job is not for the cold-hearted. He says the most important character trait for success in his job is, "A genuine interest in helping low-income and vulnerable people and, to be more specific, in empowering people to overcome whatever obstacles (whether perceived or real) are impeding their ability to engage in self-advocacy and work to improve their own lives. This requires an enormous amount of patience, creativity, compassion, and perseverance." The good parts of the job are that it is "challenging on so many levels, never boring, meaningful, and satisfying." He advises that if you're extremely organized and focused, you'll likely have better work-life balance than peers in private practice. The frustrations of the job include "working within, or against, a system with so many flaws—and one in which equal justice is but a hollow promise—can be, at times, very frustrating; and yes, the relative low pay makes it difficult to support a family." For those intending to pursue public interest work, it is worth noting that Kevin attended law school on a scholarship.

Prosecutor

Audry Nafziger, a senior deputy district attorney who graduated from law school in 1992, says there are a lot of good things about being a prosecutor.

> The pressure isn't on billing hours, but is on winning cases. To do so you must know your case better than your opponent. There is nothing like taking witnesses on the stand and crossing bad guys when they take the stand—it is so much fun. I also become a mini-expert in many different areas. As a prosecutor you get to learn about psychology/psychiatry, medicine, narcotics, cars, fraud, etc. To properly examine any expert you need to learn the area on which they will testify. Other good parts of my job are going out into the field to examine a crime scene and hanging out with cops on undercover operations.

Plus, Audry enjoys being on the side of something she believes in. "Let's face it, protecting your community by securing convictions on people who do bad things leaves most prosecutors with an aura of being a 'good' lawyer in a field that is often criticized."

Intellectual Property

Work in patents may require a bachelor or graduate level degree in a scientific field, but work in copyright and trademarks may not. If you want to go into patent litigation, a science or technical background is not required but in patent prosecution, it would be required. Also, in different areas of the country, the patent work varies. For example, in Dallas and Austin, Texas, the client base consists of cellular service providers and software companies, but in North Carolina, the pharmaceutical companies are prevalent and a background in biology (and, specifically, a PhD) might be more helpful than one in electrical engineering, according to Amanda Ellis, a legal recruiter in the Dallas area.

Civil Rights

Fara Gold, a federal prosecutor for the Department of Justice, Civil Rights Division, Criminal Section, says,

> I deal with police misconduct, human trafficking, and hate crimes. I work with the FBI and U.S. Attorneys to investigate and prosecute these crimes. There is no typical day. There is a lot of travel and the work changes on a weekly basis. If I am at my desk, I am doing a lot of research and preparing for my next case. Because of the travel, there is a big impact on social life, which impacts men and women differently. [The kind of person best suited to this work] is fair-minded, [and] should do it because they want to do it and because

they love it, not for the money. They have to be able to balance fairness and advocacy and need to be flexible in their daily lives and have to be friendly because you interact with a lot of people.

Insurance Litigation

This may involve deposing people who claim to be injured on the job (and being in court several times a week). Or, you might represent one of several homeowners who allegedly failed to maintain their property, resulting in a mudslide that injured another property. Lawsuits like this rarely go to trial because they are settled, but would involve taking a lot of depositions. Or, you might decide coverage issues—whether a liability policy applies to a certain claim. If you work in-house for an insurance company, you would be managing the work of outside attorneys and not dealing directly with the pleadings and litigation.

Bankruptcy

You might specialize in your representation of either secured lenders, trade creditors, commercial landlords, creditors' committees, trustees/examiners, corporate debtors (which can be very lucrative) or personal (usually a high-volume, flat-fee practice). Or, you might do strictly bankruptcy appeals—largely a written motion practice.

Marital and Family Law

Family law involves representing people at their most vulnerable: through divorce, adoption, custody and its aftermath. According to Kara Willig, you need people skills.

It is critical for you to be able to relate to your clients, lawyers, judges, potential fact and expert witnesses, and court personnel. People skills are of the utmost importance because it is essential to develop relationships with the professionals who will refer cases to you and work well with the people in your office.

Patience is required. What is important to your client could be considered trivial minutiae for corporate lawyers (such as what house a child stays at in the threat of a hurricane), but these are real-life issues important to your clients. Also, many people who hire lawyers are business-oriented and can cut to the chase. People getting divorced have emotionally regressed and need to feel heard—cut to the chase is not in their vocabulary, and you need to listen to them.

Especially in family law, you need to be savvy. In many situations, the other side (and sometimes your client) is just plain lying, and you need to detect it and know when something doesn't sound or look right.

You need attention to detail, endurance, and the ability to focus. You have to be able to multitask and quickly jump from one case or task to the next or be able to focus on one task for an incredibly long period of time. In one day, you could be in several meetings, take some calls, return some e-mails, draft some letters or motions, handle some preparation for an upcoming hearing or deposition, prepare some discovery, and head off to handle a deposition or meeting. Or you could spend 14 hours at one mediation. It all depends on the day.

I am a certified family mediator and a Guardian ad

litem for children. I am an adjunct professor of family law. As an attorney, I represent clients who are getting a divorce, need to change or enforce their divorce agreement, need a prenuptial agreement because they are getting married, or need a parenting and child support agreement because they are leaving a relationship that produced a child.

As a mediator, I will meet with the parties and sometimes their lawyers and assist them in coming up with solutions to resolve their case to everyone's satisfaction. As a Guardian ad litem, I represent a child's "best interest" when their parents who are breaking up cannot agree on what is best for their child, such as a time-sharing schedule. As an adjunct professor, I teach family law to upper-level law students.

[My job] is intellectually stimulating and can be emotionally and spiritually satisfying to know you changed the course of someone's life for the better. I am incredibly interested in how other people lead their lives, so I enjoy reading people's bank statements, credit card statements, or psychological evaluations. I like being asked for advice and solving problems. I like that for a large part of what I do I can attend to my clients and their cases virtually. With just a laptop and cell phone, I can work from almost anywhere. Being a family law attorney can be incredibly lucrative once you can generate your own cases and not rely on someone else to feed you work.

It is also emotionally draining. People's lives are in limbo while you are handling their cases. For some reason, a few family law attorneys become (or can become) too emotionally invested in their client's goals and, as a result, are rude and lack the professionalism seen in other areas of the law. The system is overburdened with cases and justice can take time.

If all of this is boring and you found yourself skimming through this chapter, then that's a good sign that you're considering law school for reasons that aren't internal but because of external pressure. If you are excited by one or more of the careers discussed in this chapter, then you should feel like law school is a fine choice for you—you truly want to be a lawyer.

On a personal level, say goodbye to work-free nights, weekends, holidays, and vacations. As children are not in school during these times, conflict is bound to arise and you will be disturbed. I have been tracked down while on vacation in Africa and Japan by clients with emergencies. Family law clients have few boundaries—the same technology we use to gain some freedom and flexibility can work against us too—you will be called or get texted at all hours of the night, because they rely on you to solve their problems. It is very difficult to achieve that so-called "balance" between work and a private life when you are a litigator and a family law litigator in particular.

Family law is all about networking. Every job I have ever gotten in family law has been because I knew someone who knew someone who was looking to hire, and I could back up the referral with a strong resume and good interview. I attended law school where I intended to practice law, so I could clerk during the semester and meet people in my legal community. I was asked to become an adjunct by a dean who seven years earlier had been my professor. Participating in law school activities helped also—I organized panels for clubs I belonged to that allowed me to reach out to members of the legal community.

—Kira Willig, Miami, Florida

CHAPTER 14

ALTERNATIVE CAREERS IN LAW

I F you're still with me, then something about the practice of law has enticed you to read more. If that's so, then you should know that although 72.5 percent of respondents to our survey are currently practicing law and some of the others are in academia or are judges, a number of people are in alternative legal careers and some of them stated they had never intended to practice law—even when going through law school. A few were stay-at-home parents, and others built practices as consultants in various fields or work as lobbyists. When we asked this group why they are not practicing law, the reasons fell into four categories: (1) never intended to practice law, (2) pursued another business/profession, (3) did not like it/lifestyle decision, and (4) were laid off/unable to find permanent employment. I am sharing their comments so you can evaluate what else you can do with a law degree, and the reasons why people choose to leave the practice of law.

Never Intended to Practice Law

- "I knew when I attended law school I never wanted to practice. I did practice for about 5.5 years then transitioned into a nontraditional legal career."
- "I went to law school to become a more effective lobbyist."
- "I was working in intercollegiate athletics administration and wanted to position myself to be eligible for senior level positions within my field."
- "I never wanted to be a practitioner per se, but wanted to use law in other areas."

Pursued Another Business/Profession

- "I make more money in the oil and gas industry without billable hours."
- "I lead a foundation dedicated to improving and saving lives in Africa."
- "I'm currently writing, speaking, and consulting. I keep my license active and my consulting includes legal research and writing projects, but I'm not carrying malpractice insurance."
- "I decided that I could have more impact on public interest issues via politics than as a public interest lawyer."
- "I chose to pursue a nonprofit management career because I wanted to make the world a better place, and legal skills were only part of what I wanted to use to do that."
- "I transitioned to title insurance and another real estate-related business."

- "I switched to a law-related profession."
- "I started my own company."

Of those **not** practicing law, 64 percent say their law degrees help them in their current profession. Here are some of the ways they elaborated on this statement:

- "Legal knowledge is always a plus in the nonprofit sector."
- "I work with lawyers and judges and wouldn't have the credibility I need even though I have other professional training."
- "JD required for the position."
- "I'm a feminist and community activist, writer, and public speaker, and my legal background is a great help."
- "Provides a powerful professional credential. Provides a way of strategic thinking and the ability to negotiate with partners and win over current and potential donors."
- "It always helps to have a terminal degree, and the analytical skills I've developed are priceless."
- "Provided immediate camaraderie when encountering lawyers at my firm."
- "Now in law enforcement."
- "I needed a JD for the position, but I probably could not have gotten the job on the degree alone. I needed prior Capitol Hill experience."
- "It's not required for my job, but it looked better on my resume."
- "Gave me a certain sense of perceived stature/

accomplishment despite switching into politics at 29 without a political resume."

- "I work as a litigation consultant."
- "My JD provides me with critical legitimacy when dealing with lawyers and law firms. Without it, they wouldn't listen to a word I say."
- "Having a JD and having passed a bar exam are two of the hiring criteria for my position."
- "While I knew I didn't want to practice law, I also knew I had to gain legal skills to make my valuable degree actually worth something and useful to a future employer. I also knew I wanted to stay within the legal world and to work with lawyers without actually having to *be* one. Lawyers have a mutual respect for their degrees and bar admission; it is a small-world club and having attended and graduated from law school makes me a member of the club."
- "I work on creating products and curriculum for bar exam review courses and law school curriculum. You need to have gone to law school and passed the bar exam to hold this position."
- "Not so much in entering the field but it certainly has helped me progress in my career."
- "I was already in the field, but the law degree helped me to progress into senior-level management within the field."
- "Discipline, analytical thinking improved."
- "A law degree offers credibility. My undergraduate degree was in computer science and I found that people pigeonholed me as a techie. The tech/law combination gives me business credibility."

- "Provided additional skill and ability to 'think like a lawyer.'"
- "Gave legal and practical experience in the area(s) in which I am now working."
- "I coach lawyers to have more fulfilling and successful law practices."
- "I would not have been hired for the admissions position. The JD has brought me credibility in the field and has been considered equivalent to other graduate degrees."
- "I would not have been hired without my JD."
- "The research I did in law school led to founding my company."
- "Gave me both the credentials and experience I needed for my current job."
- "Need JD for credibility."

Did Not Like It/Lifestyle Decision

- "After having worked in firms and then starting and growing my own, I realized I liked people and talking (what I do now) more than research and writing (the core of law practice). I left law and became a consultant."
- "I only practiced for three years out of law school— long enough to prove to myself that I could, but more than long enough to realize that it wasn't what I wanted."
- "It's a terrible way to make a living."
- "I grew disenchanted with practice."
- "After 18 years, it just became unfulfilling. My practice became more about paper than people. The legal

community became less collegial, with too much
negativity and incivility."

- "I hated it. Left for a business job, then became a
therapist."

Was Laid Off/Unable to Find Permanent Employment[104]

- "I was laid off from Milbank Tweed, where I practiced
finance law, in 2009, and haven't been able to find
work practicing law since."
- "The Indiana/Chicago market was overcrowded,
so I moved to DC after graduation. To date, of the
approximately 50 people from my school living here,
a handful of graduates are working as government
employees in nonlaw positions, two are working at
law firms, and the rest are contract attorneys, as am I.
It's not really the practice of law, and it doesn't provide
skills that will help transfer out of law. It's just kind of
no-man's-land of temporary gigs that pay the bills; but
we all stay because, at least for me, the student loans
have to be paid and this is the only way I can do that."
- "Only one in-school job interview and one job interview after graduation (in two years of searching after
graduation). As an evening student with a family, I
stayed with my 9-5 nonlegal job rather than try to set
up own practice in 2008."
- "The market for lawyer jobs was bad when I graduated and passed the bar in 2008 and got progressively

---

[104] Please note that these were absolutely all of the responses to this question—of 258
lawyers, these were the only comments that fell into this category.

worse. I have a business background, and my skills
in that arena were more valuable than the skills
that I honed in law school (whatever those are).
Unfortunately, I took out $150k in loans to, basically,
do the type of work I would likely have been able to
do with or without law school."[105]

The Benefit of a JD Degree in Nonlegal Careers

Almost all of the nonpracticing lawyers we interviewed
were in agreement: their law degrees bring them credibility
in their current fields. Eve Grossman-Bukowski, a graduate
of University of California-Davis, never intended to practice
law but wanted to be a more effectively lobbyist. "Attending
law school provided me with more credibility with the legis-
lators and enables me to more effectively write and analyze
legislation."

When graduating from college, Jessica Silverstein, owner of
Attorney's Counsel[106] (a resume reviewing company for attorneys) was too scared to tell her parents she didn't want to go to
law school. "I knew I wanted to be a professional and knew I
wanted an advanced degree, but knew I never really wanted to
go to court," said the graduate of Brooklyn Law School in an
interview with me. "I pursued what I wanted to do—I didn't

---

[105] Let's not make light of this situation. Several articles have been posted on blogs
claiming that there are only jobs for half of all law school graduates each year. I
confess that the math behind the analysis seems sketchy to me, and the headlines
seem designed for Tweeting. Here are some articles you may want to read: http://
abovethelaw.com/2011/06/the-oversupply-of-lawyers-in-america/#more-78975;
http://moneyland.time.com/2011/07/05/consumers-finally-figure-out-that-
law-school-is-overrated/; http://minnlawyer.com/minnlawyerblog/2011/06/27/
and-here-is-proof-that-yes-there-are-too-many-lawyers/.

[106] For more on Jessica's career path see: www.vault.com/wps/portal/usa/blogs/
entry-detail/?blog_id=1260&entry_id=12644 and www.superwomenjds.
com/2010_08_01_archive.html.

kill myself for grades because I didn't want a big firm, and I didn't have loans so I had flexibility in my career options. I did a lot of informational interviewing—I knew that I enjoyed recruiting and event planning so I talked to my friends who knew recruiters, and I would talk with them and with career counselors at Brooklyn Law. I wanted to speak to them about options for alternative legal careers; no one said, 'Oh, you could do what I do.' They all said, 'You should practice.'" This proved true when she became a legal recruiter and clients were relieved that she understood their needs and did not need to explain elementary legal tasks to her. She says:

> It was never my plan to start my own business—I would've stayed doing placement forever, but I went on maternity leave when the legal field collapsed, and there were no placements to be made. I knew it wasn't going to get better, but I was speaking all the time about doing resumes and I was helping people do this for free. My husband convinced me to start a business. I am connected with City Bar committees and I had a network of friends. I had seen thousands and thousands of resumes and started a resume review business at a time when people really needed this help.

Jessica now advises that all law school graduates practice law before pursuing an alternative legal career. She cites three reasons for this: "(1) you may try it and like it and want to continue to do it; (2) if you know you want to do something that will enable you to enjoy using your legal brain—you won't know how to do this without having practiced and you won't have these skills; and (3) lawyers trust other lawyers, for the most part."

If you are considering going to law school because you

hope to pursue a nontraditional career, talk to people in your desired career—those who have law degrees and those who do not—and ask them whether they believe a JD degree (and, if so, from which school) will assist you meaningfully in your career.

Predicting Your Future

What will you be doing in 10 years? Let's say that you'll graduate from law school between 24 and 28 years of age. Chances are that within a few years of graduation you may be thinking about marriage and starting a family. I am a feminist. I am not a stay-at-home mom (although I am a work-at-home mom). I think that most women entering law school think of a future version of themselves and see career women. It's an easy thing to picture—we dress up in suit, carry a briefcase, and have important lunches. It's much harder to envision the reality of what that life is like with kids.

Think about what you want to be doing in 10 years. That may feel like a long time from now, but time passes a lot more quickly when you don't have your progress through school to measure it. Your priorities change: you may not even be in a relationship now; however, you might be ready to get married in a year or two and then have children a few years after that. It's hard to predict when you will feel ready for each next step in life, but you still have to make decisions—leaving these possibilities open in your life. You must try to understand the impact that the decisions you make today will have on your future— your ability to get married, have children, change professions, or take a break from working should you later decide to do any or all of these things.

I recently heard an interview on NPR by a (female) doctor

who wrote a *New York Times* editorial[107] urging other female doctors to continue to actively use their training and education instead of staying home with their children. She argued that (1) they had a moral obligation to do so because there was a shortage of doctors and public resources were used in their training and education; and (2) they would not be able to return to the profession easily when their children became older. While argument #1 may not apply to lawyers, argument #2 does. If you take more than a year at a time off from your legal career, or even work part-time as a attorney (if you are lucky enough to find someone willing to employ you on that basis), it will be assumed that your skills are rusty and that you're not as "hungry."

A senior partner in the small litigation boutique firm where I was practicing told me the following: first, he had a feeling I might go on the "mommy-track" so he wasn't going to pay me what he should pay me according to my billable hours; second, because my husband was also a lawyer, I "didn't need the money." It should be noted that I wasn't even pregnant at the time, but was recently married. Yes, we have laws to protect against these forms of discrimination, but it is very difficult to take advantage of those protections for two reasons: (1) you risk burning bridges with your employer and in your legal community—so much so that another local attorney probably won't even agree to represent you against the employer; and (2) it is expensive; small employers are often exempt from laws (such as the Family Medical Leave Act), and chances of recovering anything out of the claim are minimal.

Audry Nafziger, a Senior District Attorney and graduate

---

[107] www.nytimes.com/2011/06/12/opinion/12sibert.
html?_r=2&scp=3&sq=sibert&st=cse.

of the University of Southern California, says: "I love being a lawyer; being a mom and being a lawyer is difficult. I wish I'd considered that more when in law school. For a woman who wants to have and raise her children, the legal profession is not very compatible—there are very few part-time law jobs, even in the public sector. Additionally, the stress of the job makes it hard to unwind and enjoy time with family on a day-to-day basis."[108]

I interviewed three stay-at-home mothers who previously practiced law but have no intentions to re-enter the workforce. They had three things in common: (1) they practiced law for a short amount of time (1.5 years, 2 years, and 6.5 years, respectively); (2) they had no student loan debt (one attended law school on a merit scholarship); and (3) they are married to professionals. If you believe you may want to stay home and raise a family one day, keep that in mind as you decide whether to accumulate debt—especially given the number of years you can expect to practice law before starting a family and the likelihood of having a life partner who is able to support your lifestyle on a single income.

---

[108] Telephone interview, 04/11/2011.

PART IV

BUILDING YOUR
CAREER IN LAW

*"But the person who scored well on an SAT will not
necessarily be the best doctor or the best lawyer or the best
businessman. These tests do not measure character, leadership, creativity, perseverance."*

William J. Wilson, PhD,
Lewis P. and Linda L Geyser University Professor,
Harvard University

CHAPTER 15

HOW TO PICK A LAW SCHOOL

YOU'RE still with me! That's great! It means that even with your eyes wide open about how hard you'll have to work, you are still seriously interested in applying to law school.

In *The Law School Admission Game: Play Like an Expert*, there is a chapter on selecting schools to apply to and another on deciding where to attend. In those chapters, I discussed the ramifications of choosing a law school based on what a magazine publishes, and how to get real information about how employers view the schools in the markets where you hope to work after graduating. I also included a section entitled, "A Realistic View of Taking on Debt." If, after reading *this* book, you feel ready to start thinking about applying to law school, then I highly recommend you read *that* one next.

However, the subject is so important that I don't feel I can skip it here. If we are discussing how to move forward in starting your career in law (which is absolutely what you are doing by deciding to apply to law school, and if you're not ready to say that out loud then you're probably not ready to apply), then the discussion would be incomplete without at least some guidance about how to get there. After all, you can't jump from making the decision to be a lawyer to finding your first job out of law school. Choosing a law school to attend and knowing how to take advantage of your time and the opportunities presented to you there are essential to getting yourself into the career you hope to enjoy.

According to Laurence Rose, Professor Emeritus and Director of the Litigation Skills Program, University of Miami School of Law,

> The 1L year at virtually all the schools is the same: lecture classes in bread-and-butter general law courses, with a final exam making the grade decision, and a legal writing/research class. The 2L year gives the perspectives of more areas of the law and largely statutory courses, and the 3L year is courses of specialization and experiences. Prospective students should examine the curricula of the law schools to see how they depart from the norm and expand on the opportunities to learn and experience the law they think they will practice.

Does Ranking Matter?

The answer, as in all law-related questions, is "it depends." If you are looking for an unsurpassed intellectual environment, access to a Supreme Court clerkship, or a direct route to BigLaw, then school ranking does matter. However, if these aren't your goals—or if they *are* your goals but your credentials won't merit serious consideration at the Harvards and Stanfords no matter how much you dream of attending, there needs to be another set of criteria. If, however, you would be perfectly happy staying in your home town and helping people with wills and trusts, custody arrangements, adoptions, etc., then going to a regional law school nearby will never hold you back and could certainly help as you network with your fellow classmates who will also, most likely, be staying nearby.

A law professor who attended New York University and who teaches at a law school ranked in the top 100 by *U.S. News and World Report* made the following comment, "If you know where you want to live, go to a school in that state which has the best reputation among the bar. If you get a scholarship, really consider that school, and compare the cost of attendance in making your decision: high loan amounts may affect job decisions later on. Look at the resources of the schools. Schools that have a lot of money have greater opportunities for students. Unless you get into a Top 20 school, disregard the *U.S. News* rankings."[109]

One attorney who attended Harvard says that although there is a school-snob culture in BigLaw, boutique firms and companies aren't as particular and look more to the person's experience because there isn't time to train someone on the job.

However, Deborah Epstein Henry (who attended Yale for her undergraduate work before attending Brooklyn Law School) says she sees a lot of frustration when she speaks at law schools.

> Given the spotlight on law schools right now, [if I were applying to law school] I would be very deliberate in looking realistically at where I could get into school and where their graduates are going. I see a lot of law students at second-and third-tier schools graduating with $100,000 in debt and no job prospects. You have

---

[109] I urge you not to take this cutoff too literally. After all, rankings change from year to year. Use this (and other ballparks including "Top 14" or "Top 10") as an approximate range.

to look at whether you can afford to take this risk, and if you can't get into a school with better returns, you need to consider whether law school is the appropriate choice.

There is, of course, more to picking a law school than job prospects alone: campus environment, responsiveness of faculty/administration to student needs, cost of attendance, availability of jobs, and—of course—location are all part of the consideration. For purposes of our discussion, we'll restrict ourselves to this (for more, see Chapter 17 of *The Law School Admission Game*).

In Chapter 7, we ranked the lawyers' responses to important factors in choosing a law school (see Figure 7.1). Here, we highlight the most popular factors lawyers said were "very important":

1. Location near job and internship opportunities (74%)
2. Bar passage rate (72%)
3. Supportiveness of faculty and administration (69%)
4. *U.S. News* rankings (67%)
5. Cost of attendance; Area of specialization (tied) (55%)

I understand that a prominent school of thought on message boards is to go to a Top 10 law school or don't bother going at all. People who believe that, and whose accomplishments put them in that category, may take issue with this section of the book. Certainly, there are doors that open if you go to a Top 5 law school that wouldn't otherwise open. Martha Kimes, a graduate of Columbia, says: "In my own experience, the ranking of where I went to school made 100 percent difference in the opportunities I was given and where I ended up in my career path—especially if you're looking for a BigLaw job (which certainly helps you pay down student loans)." However, there are some short-term downsides to attending an elite school. "Theoretically, it's a far superior education but what you need in practice, to take the bar, to actually go represent the client . . . . All these other people around me had taken these practical classes, maybe they were offered at Columbia and I just didn't take them, but I felt I was facing all sorts of things I hadn't seen or thought." One of my close friends (a graduate of Yale) told me the same thing.

I have seen a lot of attorneys who do good work, lead good lives, and make good money who went to mediocre law schools (or law schools that conventional wisdom puts in the "crappy" category). I think a lot of life is what you make of it. So, I asked lawyers, "Do you feel as though you could have attended a lesser ranked law school and had the same career?" There were 59 percent who answered "yes." (It should be noted that graduates of Harvard, Stanford, and University of Chicago were among them.) When asked "Do you regret not attending a higher-ranked school?" 74 percent said "no" (and only 23 percent of respondents attended schools in the Top 15).

"[The] law school experience tends to be fairly similar across the board: very uniform curriculum, professors at all schools are outstanding, you are going to get the law school experience no matter where you go," said one attorney at BigLaw who graduated from the University of San Francisco.

> You are going to have the opportunity no matter what; success is about taking advantages of the opportunities presented to you not about what law school you go to." "When I interview a candidate, I am not focused on what law school did you go to. I look for experience, relevant experience, and whether they have done the work that is relevant. In a broad sense, that is how

I got to BigLaw by lateral transfer after 12 years of experience: I had amassed a huge amount of relevant experience, and it was not about where I went to law school, it was what I did after law school.

However, another attorney, a graduate of the University of Michigan, disagreed. "Law school is a door opener. Go to the best-ranked law school you get into." (However, when asked whether she regretted not attending a higher ranked law school, she said "no.") Andrew Flusche attended University of Virginia and says, "UVA Law is a great school, and I think it prepared me well to be an excellent attorney. However, it doesn't have any focus on starting or running a firm. Most graduates end up at BigLaw firms, and that's how career services is oriented. I'm glad I chose UVA, but I'm sure there are other schools that provide a solid education and can help the students get their own firm up and running."

A lawyer who graduated from the University of Texas in 2000 thinks he hit the perfect middle ground in choosing a law school. As a Texas resident, he attended a Top 20/15 law school (depending on the year) and came out of law school with minimal debt (which he paid off within five years of graduation).

However, I would not have had the same career if I had not been in the top of my class. It is important for students to consider that the lower ranked the school, the higher ranked you must be in your class, and that the higher ranked the school, the less important class rank is. One mistake a lot of law students make is that they go to a second tier but very expensive law school when they would be better off trying to spend the same money on a better-ranked school, or spend a fraction on a lower-ranked school.

One attorney, who attended a Top 100 school but works in BigLaw, still regrets his choice of school. He advises applicants to go where there are more opportunities and connections and real big players. "Look at the type of people who will be in that law school. You may be motivated wherever you go, but that doesn't mean everyone where you go will be motivated, and the higher you go more likely people will be more motivated. The higher ranked law school has the advantage of being more of a door opener to develop than a lower ranked law school." Another lawyer, however, said "Attending a higher ranked school may open doors, but you still have to walk the walk."

Brandon Scheele, an attorney in Tampa, Florida, says location is very important in choosing a law school.

> I think it is crucial unless you go to a [name brand] school (Notre Dame or Stanford looks awesome on a resume no matter what); however, if you are going to a middle-of-the-road school, you have to go local. You make contacts at law school and work at local law firms, and you don't make those contacts when you go out of state unless family members introduce you. And it makes the bar exam a lot easier.

Another reason to go to law school near where you hope to practice law is that some of the country's top law schools may not offer adequate courses in the specialties that interest you. Leon Liu shared his experience. "At Harvard, an East-Coast school, my entertainment law class dealt mostly with rights of publicity, press issues, newspaper stuff, defamation. At UCLA, I'm sure the entertainment law courses are more on-point because of immediate access to the industry." Of course, just going to Harvard opened doors to firms that garnered him experience in his chosen field; but for others, it may be important to choose a school that offers relevant courses in your intended field(s) of law.[110] However, don't choose a law school just because it offers one specialty and for no other reason: in the end you might not like that specialty or you might find yourself unemployable because your experience is too narrow.

---

[110] For more on Leon's career trajectory, see Chapter 13.

CHAPTER 16

HOW TO SPEND
YOUR TIME DURING
LAW SCHOOL

THE old standbys of good grades and law review really only result in employment for those headed to BigLaw (or getting hired by those who share BigLaw values). For everybody else, finding your way into a law career will take initiative and will require you to be proactive.

Kira Willig, a family law attorney, mediator, and adjunct law professor, offers this advice and insights about achieving academic success in law school:

> Take classes based on the professor, not the subject matter. Don't goof off on the Internet during class and say you will catch up during reading period. If you can't concentrate when you are paying to be there, no prospective employer will want you to learn how to concentrate when other people are paying you to do work. Lose the attitude of entitlement and learn how to engage in self-help. I am consistently surprised and disappointed with the attitude of law students or new lawyers that they are entitled to anything without first

paying their dues, or ask me questions because it is easier to ask me than to look it up on their own. I also expect that if a student, law clerk, or new lawyer comes to me with a problem, they are also coming to me with a potential solution and a willingness to help solve the problem. If you can't do that, you shouldn't be a lawyer.

Brandon Scheele emphasizes the importance of moot court and mock trial for those who hope to be litigators because this is the closest thing in law school to what a lawyer actually does. He also recommends shadowing attorneys. For those of you who might be intimidated to ask lawyers for this opportunity, you should know that many lawyers are willing to do it. "If somebody calls me and asks to come along with me for the day, I would let them do it. I think it's important. You might think you want to be a family lawyer and then after a day you spend seeing people fighting over their kids you'll learn that you don't want to do that. You could call people and interview them to talk about it."

One experience that is almost universally helpful is spending your year after graduation as a law clerk. This is something you have to start thinking about as a 2L but, according to Chris Kratovil, who clerked for Judge Judith Jones of the Fifth Court of Appeals and is now a partner at K&L Gates in Dallas, Texas, "a judicial clerkship is absolutely very important. It's similar to a medical residency or finishing school for young lawyers." He says he gained a valuable learning experience, a mentor, and a prestigious position for his resume.

During my first summer, I received a public interest grant to work at Legal Aid where I got to interact with clients and do more than write research memos. The next year, when class rankings came out and I learned I was in the top 10 percent of my class, I felt pressure from the career services office to participate in on-campus interviews even though I felt I didn't have the personality to survive in BigLaw. I wanted to work in employment law, and so I thought learning the defense side would only help me. I knew I didn't want to stay in Miami after graduation (I know, stupid, stupid girl!), so I flew myself to a job consortium in Atlanta. I received call-backs to big firms that flew me to their cities to interview, and I split my summer between two cities and two firms. I thought I was playing it safe by hedging my bets, but in hindsight it probably would've made me more hirable to be really dedicated to one city and one firm and become more invested. After that summer, I was really burned out on BigLaw and decided to change my focus. I took family law courses, an intensive family law seminar, a family law internship, and a clerkship. I decided I was going to completely change what I wanted to do. I never had a problem getting interviews—I interviewed everywhere from the Department of Justice to the Army JAG Corps to labor law firms, etc. The combination of my grades and experiences (and evidence that I was generally hardworking) always seemed to impress people. However, I was scattered. I didn't know what I wanted to do—I only knew I was a litigator rather than a deal-maker.

In the end, I felt overwhelmed and used all of my student leadership experience to talk my way into a job at the University of Denver College of Law, thus beginning my career in higher education. This happened to be the right career for me, and I stopped floundering and started flourishing. My diverse internship experiences in law school proved valuable in my ability to relate to the students I worked with, and my leadership experience in law school served as my de facto internships for a career in higher education.

When I was in law school, I was all about racking up the activities: law review was for resume building (trust me, there is no pleasurable reason to join law review), but the Student Bar Association, the Jewish Students Association, the Public Interest Law Group—I joined those because I was interested in them and not because I thought they'd help me get a job. In some ways, I was interesting to employers because I'd demonstrated some leadership experience. However, the people who were really smart chose their activities according to which would enable them to encounter practicing lawyers. I should have spent that time forming relationships within those organizations, not just racking up improvements at the law school and feeling self-satisfied at being such a standout. Instead of being friends with my professors because I liked them, I should have used those relationships to build other relationships and asked, "Who can you introduce me to who practices labor law?"

Making connections with your classmates is also important—don't just show up for class and leave campus. "Another key to success in law school that lays the foundation for future career satisfaction is to make friends."[111] I still keep in touch with many friends from law school (thanks to Facebook, mostly, since I live far away from where I attended law school). These are some of my biggest supporters. Two law school friends live nearby and we are able to have lunch or dinner occasionally and help promote each other's career-related efforts or just serve as sounding boards for each other. I encourage you to make friends during law school with an eye to creating a lifelong

---

[111] Nancy Levit and Douglas O. Linder, *The Happy Lawyer: Making a Good Life in the Law* (Oxford University Press, 2010), 133.

network of mutual support and encouragement. My brother, who is 10 years out of law school, recently got married. Out of six groomsmen, four were friends from law school.

I asked Doug Linder and Nancy Levit, both of whom are law professors, "How can students take responsibility for finding their own job paths rather than relying on a "standard" career services office-driven path?" Nancy recommended that students look for different programs or colloquia or symposia in their area of interest.

> The students who are most successful in finding a job in their areas of interest pay attention to what's appearing in blogs, symposia going on at a different law school nearby, and they talk to the lawyers who attend those programs. They read up on innovations in related fields, breaking out of what is given at the law school in terms of programming, and finding those specialized programs, networks, or contacts outside. One student really wanted to go into health law, and her grades alone wouldn't have qualified her for the larger employers who typically do the work. She read the Health Insurance Portability and Accountability Act (HIPAA) regulations, wrote independent study papers on health law, made lots of phone calls to many lawyers and met with them to ask them about their practices, started a health law society at her school, and is now working in that area—she created her job.

Outside the walls of the law school, internships are absolutely vital. You must leave the campus and experience the legal world in practice as Noah Solomon advises in the following:

> The first step for anyone wanting to enter this field, while

in law school, is to get internships. That's a key: you're showing a demonstrable interest, learning the business, meeting people. All of that is extremely important in getting ahead: getting an internship and impressing your mentor and supervisor. While I was working in Legal Affairs at ABC, I restarted the paid internship program because I wanted to give kids a leg-up that's not always available, and I love to teach—I'm constantly going to Southwestern and speaking in classes or on panels.

When looking at applicants for internships, I look at whether the person has shown a demonstrated interest in entertainment. You can whittle down 100 applicants to three or four immediately. Part of that is the catch-22: how do you show demonstrated interest? Some were in entertainment in some form before law school, through involvement in theatre, etc. If somebody comes from LA, I'm not going to necessarily [infer that they did so to be near the entertainment industry], but if someone comes from across the country to go to an LA school, then I think the implication is that they came here because of what this region is going to give them. Law schools are fairly regional in their focus. You go to school in the Bay Area and you're not from there, the implication is you want to work in the tech industry. What [a job or internship applicant does] in school is second tier after internship/previous industry experience. [Participation in the] Entertainment and Sports Law Society shows interest, but I'll look at somebody who has taken it on themselves to get their foot in the door [first]. I am more interested in dedicated entertainment experience than law firm experience. You get a lot of people who have

preconceived notions about whether law firm experience
is beneficial—Disney wants someone out of a law firm
and is not going to hire someone who didn't work at a
good firm.

I never worked at a law firm. I had a boss who
immediately dinged anyone without law firm experience, even though he agreed that I was [perfectly
qualified]. I wanted to know why [that was necessary]
if they've proven themselves otherwise. I interviewed
years ago with the head of legal affairs there for two
jobs—one on network side and one on studio side. I
interviewed with 12 people in one day; I knew a few
people there and I came recommended. I was offered
the network job, but it was a consultant position
working on Kimmel and might not be permanent.
[The person who hired me] understood when I didn't
take it. Later, I contacted her and she had a job for me.

There's some school snobbery that goes on, but
I got hired because people knew me and liked me.
Another time, I was at Universal looking for a jump.
There was an opening at Universal Music Group and
I had someone contact the hiring manager. Objections
weren't that I didn't know music, but that I didn't
go to UCLA or better. I wasn't even given a courtesy
interview through a mutual friend even though I was
an internal candidate. It happens. It hasn't been a bar
to success. That's not somebody I'd want to work
for anyway. Unless you go to Harvard and have a
wonderful pedigreed firm, you won't have an easy in
to the industry. There are other ways in—I started as
an assistant for a year and did that with the head of

business affairs at Universal TV because the guy who did it before me gave me an informational interview and he went to Southwestern.

> —Noah Solomon, Vice President
> of Legal Affairs for BBC and a graduate
> of Southwestern School of Law

I always tell my law school admission consulting clients that no one will hand them a job upon law school graduation—no matter where they attend. You're going to have to work for everything you've got. Even good grades and law review and moot court aren't going to help unless you market yourself. I've seen too many law students become bitter about how the career placement offices at their schools "only" serve the top 10 percent of the class. Be your own career adviser—be in charge of your own life and you will find opportunities. I think this is a pretty universal philosophy. So, if you're used to other people figuring things out for you, you're going to have a tough time in law school and in the job market.

Start thinking about building your career—that means considering what you want to do, what law school you need to attend to get there, and what you can do during law school to increase the likelihood that you'll be on the right path to get there. In this chapter we discuss the benefits of working in a law-related field prior to law school. There are also benefits to working in other fields. "I worked at a big tech company prior to law school. This experience helped me learn to navigate the corporate world and deal with a variety of personalities," said Josh Banerje, a graduate of the University of Chicago. "In a way it was just helpful to be in an office environment, sitting at a desk, being in conference calls, and seemingly endless meetings."

Currently an associate with Pillsbury Winthrop Shaw Pittman's San Francisco office, this was great preparation for life in BigLaw.

An attorney with the Federal Energy Regulatory Commission advises law students to be prepared and be persistent: "Get as much experience as possible and knock on every door. I begged for jobs that didn't pay and sent out 10 requests a day for informational interviews while in law school. I did a different internship every semester and contacted any alum that I thought did anything that sounded remotely interesting. When I didn't get a response from someone, I sent up to three follow-up e-mails. People are willing to help; you just have to reach out to them." Today the tables are turned, and she interviews law students and prospective lawyers for employment with the Commission. "I am always amazed at how many students come into the interview knowing nothing and completely unprepared to discuss even the general topics we work on." She also sees other basic mistakes. "[I often see] glaring typos that scream lack of attention to detail. Even if you don't want the job, act like you are interested in what someone else does; it might lead to a discussion that opens up an aspect you might find very interesting."

When asked how they got their first jobs out of law school, the winner, at 31 percent, was networking and professional contacts. An equal number got jobs through on-campus interviews and responding to job postings, and slightly fewer through summer associate positions. Figure 16.1 shows that you really need to take initiative to find a job because on-campus interviews and summer associate offers together account for only 42 percent of all postgraduate job offers.

Figure 16.1 **How did you get your first job out of law school?
Please check all that apply.**

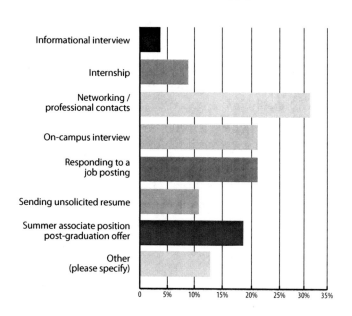

I highly recommend *The 6Ps of the BIG 3 for Job-Seeking JDs: 60+ Ways to Get Hired Using Social Networking* (Dallas, TX: Something Different Publishing, 2010) by Amanda Ellis. It provides concrete tips and strategies (with "how to" screen shots and examples) for using social media to network as a law student and lawyer. She has some great examples of people who used social networking tools like Twitter and LinkedIn to build connections that ultimately led to dream jobs as lawyers.[112]

Open-ended responses to this question ("How did you find your first job out of law school?") included references to

---

[112] http://solopracticeuniversity.com/2001/02/10/how-to-land-your-dream-job/.

career services offices and clerkship/fellowship application processes. A few respondents also said they opened their own law firms or businesses right after law school. Other responses and comments included:[113]

- "Clerkship—I sent out lots of resumes."
- "Worked for my father's law practice."
- "Sending unsolicited resume to firm that I currently work for."
- "Was recommended by law school classmate."
- "I got my job through on-campus interviews. But while waiting to start work in 2001, they offered everyone six months of severance to please give up their offers due to the Silicon Valley downturn. I got a job at Jones Day just a few weeks later through submission of a resume because they were opening their office in Silicon Valley and needed a first year."
- "I served as a briefing attorney on an appellate court then worked for a litigation boutique in Houston, Texas."
- "Ran my family's nonprofit foundation."
- "I had a friend in marketing who called every law firm in Fort Wayne, Indiana, trying to sell them on hiring me as an intern. It worked."
- "Started own firm."
- "Hired full time after a temporary assignment.
- "Entered moot court competition."
- "My first 'job' was an internship with a Senator's office on the Hill."
- "Volunteered for an alumnus while in law school

---

[113] I am listing all these to provide ideas for you—things you can do to find your own jobs. Get out your highlighter!

and then went to work for him full-time after passing the bar."

- "Worked for same employer I was working with during my third year in law school."
- "Foundation Fellowship— I was selected to be one of 20 top grad students nationally for a fellowship to start a nonprofit organization. I turned down law firm offers and a U.S. District Court clerkship to do this."
- "My first job was working for a professor of mine who holds a position at the U.N. I did that for six months before moving to Chile."
- "Specifically, I met my current boss (named partner) through a law school closing argument competition against another state school. My boss coached the team from my school. We won; I made a favorable impression and courting followed."
- "Was referred by a friend."
- "Was working as a clerk at a firm."
- "Did contract work for five years before getting first permanent position" (this person graduated from Fordham within the last 6 to10 years and would not recommend that anyone go to law school because of the competitiveness of the job market, but she does say she enjoys a rich personal life, takes vacations often enough, and is able to take care of her family even though she works part time and makes "slightly less" than the median attorney salary).
- "Still working at same position as when I was in law school."
- "I was a paralegal in the firm prior to and during law school."

- "Was promoted from student worker to full time at my current job during law school and have been here ever since."

On my Blog Talk Radio Show, "Job Prospects and Law School Rankings," I interviewed three 1Ls. Although their law schools ranged from Top 10 (Berkeley) to #39 (Hastings) to Third Tier (McGeorge), all three women had jobs lined up for the summer. Not one of them got their job through on-campus interviewing; each took initiative and it paid off.[114]

My favorite story about taking initiative comes from Noah Solomon, who as a student at Southwestern School of Law, went to the development office at his law school and got a list of all of the school's alumni working in the entertainment industry. He then wrote to each one, asking for an informational interview, and then followed up with a phone call. "I got a ton of great information from people who responded." Noah said this led him to his first job in the industry. "I interviewed [one of the attorneys] to find out what he did; I didn't even know he was interviewing me to replace him because he'd been promoted. It was only an assistant level position, but I had this person who had done it before, been successful (promoted), and a year later I got promoted. It's not a common way of getting there. A lot of people work as assistants and don't go anywhere, but it does work in a lot of examples." My favorite part of Noah's story, however, is this: whenever he talks to law students, he tells them about getting the names of alumni and how it paid off. However, he has *never* received a letter from any student doing the same thing. (I asked him to let me know if anyone contacts

---

[114] www.blogtalkradio.com/ann-levine/2011/02/28/
job-prospects-and-law-school-rankings.

him for an informational interview after reading this book, so please don't let me down!) He makes a great point:

> Do the footwork—so many students want the footwork done for them. In entertainment, nothing will be handed to you. So many people in this industry had to fight and scrape and scratch their way up. You have to pay your dues and put in your time. There are a lot of smart people in this industry because competition is so fierce—people are really bright and knowledgeable about what they do. If you're not willing to do the work and learn and show ability and smarts—how will you survive? So many students think it's easy, sexy to be in entertainment. It's contracts, they think, "how hard is that?"

More than ***150 respondents said the law school they attended helped, yet only 86 of those respondents say they went to a Top 20 law school.*** It is important to remember that people did not have to choose just one answer to the question, *What factors do you think positively impacted your employability for your first job after law school?* Almost all lawyers who responded felt that it was a combination of things that increased their employability upon graduation (see Figure 16.2). It's also interesting to note the lawyers' healthy egos, as evidenced by the number of people who reported that their "good personality," "general smarts," "good interviewing skills," "confidence," and/ or "personal charm" made them employable.

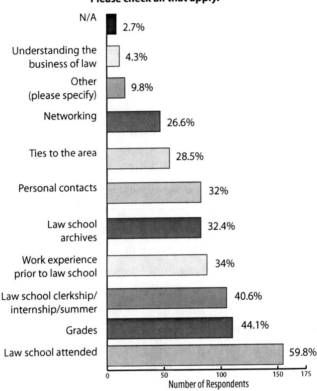

Figure 16.2 **What factors do you think positively impacted your employability for your first job after law school? Please check all that apply.**

Other responses included:

- "Luck/right place at the right time."
- "Accounting degree/CPA."
- "LLM in Taxation."
- "Maturity, language skills, willingness to take a job that paid below par."
- "I think that the partner who hired me concluded that

my personality and overall experience fit the firm's needs."

- "I had mediocre grades; it was mostly the law school [University of Chicago]. It matters more than it should."
- "Maturity and conducted a strong interview and got along well with the person who interviewed me."
- "Law school clinical experience."
- "Prestigious undergrad institution and lots of extras on my resume: Eagle Scout, National Merit, undergrad student government."
- "Work experience during law school."
- "I really have no idea: I only lasted three months, which was two months longer than the secretarial pool bet I would" (response from a lawyer who has now been practicing for more than 20 years).
- "Status of the first firm I worked for."
- "Choice of classes."

Networking played an even bigger role in how lawyers found the jobs where they are currently employed (see Figure 16.3). This shows that the lawyers you meet in practice end up being the people who help you make your next moves.

Many who responded opened their own law firms, either on their own or by joining with partners from their previous firms. Other responses included:

- "Personal contacts."
- "I accepted invitations to speak on certain topics pertinent to those who would be potential clients (professionals with license/disciplinary challenges)."

- "There is a 'meat market' for legal academics run by the American Association of Law Schools."
- "Contacted by recruiter."

Figure 16.3 **If not already addressed above, how did you find your current job? Please check all that apply.**

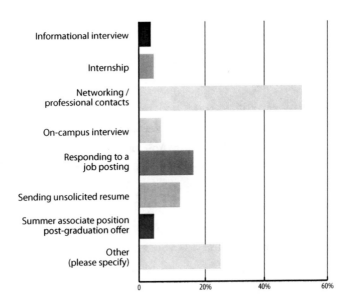

- "Networking led me to a headhunter who placed me at my current firm."
- "Referral through family contact."
- "Worked for this firm in the past. A year after I left, the managing partner made me an offer I couldn't refuse."
- "Recruited from prior firm."
- "Nepotism."
- "My husband was in practice in this area of law and

connected me with a law firm that was looking to hire an associate."

- "I have created my own job. But it would not have been possible without many professional contacts that have supported me in the endeavor."
- "Client of the firm offered a position internally."
- "Friend told me about his employer and recommended me."
- "Partner left my old firm and asked me to join him at his new firm."

Professional contacts are vital to employment after law school, and this is not something you should start working on when you're ready to find a job. You can be working on this right now—even before you begin law school—and continue to build relationships starting on your first day of law school orientation. You should be making friends, treating people respectfully, and seeking out opportunities to interact with lawyers in your community. If you simply rely on the career services office at your law school to manage your interview schedule and help you network, you're missing out on the most direct outlet to a job: *your own legwork.*

CHAPTER 17

CHOOSING AN AREA
OF SPECIALIZATION

FIRST, it's important to understand that just because you've decided to go to law school, it doesn't mean you need to know what kind of lawyer you want to be. There is no reason to "declare a major" in law school. Of the lawyers who responded to our survey, 39 percent had no specific area of law in mind when they started law school. If an area of specialization does not naturally occur to you based on your educational or professional background or personal passions, that's absolutely fine. "If a person does not have an idea of an area of specialty before law school, that is *very ok*," declared one law professor. "Law school helps to refine that process, and many do not know [what their specialty will be] until they enter practice." During law school, explore different areas by attending lectures on campus sponsored by various student groups and choose varied classes—not just subjects that are on the bar exam. Only 7 percent of the survey respondents decided they were not well suited or qualified for their intended areas; taking time to explore this during law school will give you time to develop other interests within the law.

There are two schools of thought on whether to choose an area of specialization before or during law school. Developing an area of interest can help you differentiate yourself to employers. Getting involved in journals, student organizations, community bar organizations, and writing for blogs related to these issues can get you noticed, show you're a mover and a shaker, and get you taken seriously by the contacts you encounter along the way. However, you need to be pretty darn sure that particular area of practice is what you want to do because you will feel pretty foolish applying for an insurance defense position in a mid-size firm if all you've done is entertainment law or wills and trusts.

For some lawyers, choosing their area of specialization is a way to put their personal passions into play in their career. Such is the case with Bret Stone, who graduated from Chicago-Kent College of Law in 1997. "I was on a path to become an environmental lawyer for a long time. I was an Environmental Studies major as an undergraduate. I chose my law school based on its renowned Environmental and Energy Law program. I'm passionate about environmental issues in my personal life, so for me I'm just helping clients do the same." Bret brings the point home—he practices law in an area he is passionate about, and he cites this as the reason for his overall satisfaction with his career.

There are a lot of creative ways to do this. Erica Strump is a good example. "I love the fact that I have been able to combine my passion for health, fitness, and supplements with my career—I was General Counsel at Bodybuilding.com, the largest online retailer of dietary supplements and General Counsel at VPX/Redline, a dietary supplement company."

Federal prosecutor Fara Gold started out in advocating for survivors of rape. "As an undergrad, I wanted to do social work, but a professor told me that I should be a prosecutor because I would be able to get more done that way. I went to law school with that specific goal and was very focused on that goal. I attended law school as part of a public interest-based scholarship program. I did a clinical internship the summer before my third year where I interned in a misdemeanor domestic violence unit and experienced life as state prosecutor." This led to her current position in the Criminal Section of the Department of Justice Civil Rights Division.

> Even if you have already identified a way to put your passion into practice, keep an open mind in law school. Not everyone who goes to law school with a particular area of practice in mind goes on to practice in that area. Sometimes law school introduces you to new things that interest you or you may learn that the legal market is extremely competitive in the specialty you'd hoped to pursue. One New York solo practitioner told us he thought he would go to law school to be a sports agent working in intellectual property but "had no idea what that meant and was not able to get there from law school. I studied other fields in law school, including employment law, and have pursued that."

Most lawyers who responded to our survey developed an area of specialization based on what they were introduced to in the first few years after graduating from law school. Martha Kimes began her career in insurance litigation in BigLaw and there found her niche in "soft" intellectual property law; she is now in-house counsel for GoDaddy.com. She says:

> I bounced around after I graduated and did the default thing by going into the big law firm. [You may remember Ms. Kimes from Chapter 3 as someone

who also chose to go to law school as a default option.]
Initially, I was doing insurance litigation that was
not terribly exciting. I ended up falling into doing
intellectual property work. Once I found a niche for
myself that held my interest a lot more, I really stayed
involved in that. That's where my primary focus is: soft
IP and Internet-related work. I don't have a scientific
background, and a lot of people who go into IP have
a scientific or engineering background. What I do is
copyright and trademark, so it's not necessary.

The idea of "falling" into an area of specialization was
repeated by many of our survey respondents. A few respondents were no longer practicing law (some identified themselves
as stay-at-home parents), but others gave these insights about
why they are in a different area of practice than they initially
planned. I share them with you because there are definitely
lessons to be learned from their experiences:

- "Opportunities to do so not available at my firm."
- "Area was not taught in law school and still is not, to a
  large extent."
- "Planned to go into entertainment law when I went
  to law school, but discovered I was drawn to mental
  health law."
- "I liked public interest better than government work,
  which was what I envisioned myself doing when
  applying to law school."
- "More personal freedom."
- "Developed different interests."
- "After working as a management consultant for several
  years before law school doing mergers and acquisitions, I intended to continue as an attorney; but, I

found transactional work to be much more boring and detail-oriented as an attorney, so I switched to litigation."

- "When I went to law school, I went with the idea of going into private practice in a small firm. I later changed my mind due to life experiences."

- "I wanted to work for the District Attorney, but there was a hiring freeze so I fell into bankruptcy and then workers compensation."

- "Was interested in this area but thought I would go into personal injury. Ended up in an awful personal injury firm, switched to commercial litigation."

- "Boredom."

- "Found an area that I preferred more."

- "Decided lawyers can't change the law—only politicians do that."

- "Law doesn't accommodate my area of specialization—namely strongly ethical business development consulting."

- "Went into law school thinking I would do child advocacy but clerked one summer for Los Angeles County Children's Court and found the work very difficult emotionally."

- "Took a job at a general practice firm, then the bankruptcy guy quit. I became the bankruptcy guy. If you would have told me in my first year of law school that I would spend 10 years as a bankruptcy attorney, I probably would have taken a swing at you."

- "It happens. Moved to area for life style; job offered didn't entail working in the specialty I had originally planned."

- "My interests changed during my summer associateship."
- "Family, lifestyle choice; priorities changed."
- "Was ready for a change from death penalty defense work."
- "Did not know about it."
- "When I graduated law school with a certificate of specialty in ocean resources and coastal law (environmental law), all of the paying jobs were for the 'bad guys,' and I refused to work for them."
- "I was working in real estate, which is what I focused on in law school. I hope to return to that ASAP. Right now, I'm working in the transportation industry, which is the closest position to real estate that I could find."
- "Hated entertainment law when I did it."
- "Found something more interesting."
- "I realized that I wanted to spend more time with my family, and my current job allows me to do so. My former job was at a big firm, but the hours were too much.
- "More education [needed] about specialized areas of practice."
- "I intended to be a traditional litigator maybe in criminal defense or some plaintiff's work. I found that international human rights law really captured my attention and felt like I could make a bigger difference by practicing in that field. There are lots of litigators out there. There are a lot fewer international human rights attorneys, and I still get to use a lot of my advocacy and litigation skills."

- "I do practice plaintiff's personal injury as planned. I also do a lot of commercial litigation, which I did not plan on. I also work a lot in the field of labor and employment, which I never expected. I do this because I was able to land a large police union as a client early in my career thanks to a family connection. I do the work because it is interesting, pays, and is my own."
- "Changed my mind."
- "Life takes turns."
- "New opportunities opened for me which I had not anticipated or previously been exposed to."

As you can see, a few respondents addressed the lack of availability of positions in the field they initially chose as a reason why they did not pursue it. If you evaluate the market and choose an area of specialization that is "hot" at the time, then this can market you really well as you seek employment, according to Jaret Davis, Co-Managing Shareholder of Greenberg Traurig in Miami, Florida.[115] Thirty percent of our survey respondents took a job in a field other than their intended area of interest because that's what they could get. Mona Stone says, "To the extent you develop a specialty, it can benefit you if you develop the client base. Pick a specialty early and start making connections with people who will help you build your practice."

---

[115] www.blogtalkradio.com/ann-levine/2010/11/17/how-to-get-hired-as-a-rookie-attorney.

CONCLUSION

AFTER spending 15 years thinking about these issues and six months talking to lawyers while writing this book, here are the ideas I hope you will walk away with.

- **Your First Job Is Never Your Dream Job.** It's very rare that someone is going to hand you a ground-breaking case right out of law school, so you can't expect to feel like you're saving the world right out of the gate. Jobs as first-year lawyers are still entry-level jobs. You don't start with murder trials at the district attorney's office, or with major arbitrations or mergers and acquisitions at a firm. You need to earn your way to the more exciting cases. You have to crawl before you can walk. "The best predictor of job satisfaction is age," said Tom W. Smith, head of the polling center at the University of Chicago. Smith said, "People in their fifties are usually the most gratified by their work, as they have found a field they do well in, have been promoted, and are given a degree of autonomy on the job."[116] The same is true in every field—construction, engineering, journalism, medicine, business, or teaching. You have to start at the bottom to get anywhere. Law is no different.

---

[116] www.washingtonpost.com/wp-dyn/content/article/2010/01/05/AR2010010503977.html.

- **Find a Way to "Practice Your Passions" and You Will Be a Happier Lawyer.** If you pick a practice of law that allows you to help others or be creative with your work (which isn't difficult because being a good lawyer involves thinking outside the box to find solutions for your clients), you are more likely to be happy. "The happiest workers are people in helping professions or doing creative work." Smith said, "Firefighters, clergy, and physical therapists are most likely to describe themselves as very satisfied with their work, along with people in jobs that involve caring for, teaching, and protecting others."[117]

- **Lawyers Make Good Money.** If $100,000 a year doesn't sound like a lot to you, then you might need a reality check. After all, each of the top 10 highest-paying professions—lawyer ranks as #6 when all medical-related professions are combined—pays just above the six-figure mark. The only nonmedical people who make more are CEOs and engineering managers ($140,000), airline pilots ($134,000), and then lawyers ($110,000).[118] It should be noted that all of these require advanced degrees (and, presumably, student loan debt).

- **Lawyers Enjoy a Good Quality of Life.** According to an exclusive study by *National Jurist* magazine, recent law school graduates, on average, have more disposable income than they did 10 years ago

---

[117] Ibid.

[118] www.askmen.com/money/career_150/177d_career.html.

despite higher student loan debt and a worsened job market.[119]

- **A Good Scholarship Means Freedom to Make Your Own Career Choices.** Starting salaries at smaller firms tend to range from $40,000 to $65,000, while large firms' salaries range from $145,000 to $160,000. Although the salaries at the low end increase, you will be better off if you make your career choices based on what you enjoy doing and how you want to live your life rather than by what will allow you to pay down your debt.

- **Not All Debt Is Bad.** As observed in the medical profession (where 8 out of 10 of the highest earners are), "While the profession can be lucrative, it is certainly not easy or cheap: more than 80 percent of medical-school graduates carry a debt."[120]

- **Don't Be a Job Snob: Smaller Firms Have a Lot to Offer.** Small firms (2 to 10 lawyers) represented 39.1 percent of all private practice jobs taken by the class of 2010. This was up from 7.5 percent from 2008.[121] Fifty-three percent of law firm jobs filled by graduates of the class of 2010 were at firms with 50 or fewer attorneys—7 percent higher than for the class of 2009 graduates.

---

[119] www.nationaljurist.com/content/
recent-law-grads-enjoy-better-standard-living-10-years-ago.

[120] www.askmen.com/money/career_150/177d_career.html.

[121] www.nationaljurist.com/node/820.

The Ultimate Question

This shouldn't be a default or a pressure-based decision. Go to law school

- if you are sincerely interested,
- if you are willing to take the initiative to make your own career, and
- if you are ready to work hard.

Law is a good profession. ***But, remember this:*** to be satisfied with your career in any field, you need to make choices within that field that are right for you. Just as a brilliant high school teacher might be a horrible kindergarten teacher (and vice versa), finding a niche within law that fits with your personality, work habits, and areas of interest is vital to both success and enjoyment in your life and career. ***And by all means, don't forget:*** If you are not constricted by excessive student debt, you will be freer to find this niche.

ABOUT THE AUTHOR

ANN K. Levine, Esq., is the author of the bestselling book, *The Law School Admission Game: Play Like an Expert,* available as a book and audio book. She is the owner and Chief Consultant for LawSchoolExpert.com, a company she established in 2004. Since that time, Ann has assisted hundreds of law school applicants through the admission process and nearly 100,000 people read her Law School Expert blog each year.

After graduating magna cum laude from the University of Miami School of Law, Ann served as Director of Student Services at the University of Denver College of Law, as Director of Admissions for California Western School of Law, and as Director of Admissions for Loyola Law School in Los Angeles. She (briefly) practiced law in Colorado and California before opening Law School Expert.

Ann lives in Santa Barbara, California, with her husband (an attorney) and their two daughters. When she is not helping people get into law school, she is playing tennis. You can follow Ann on Twitter @annlevine and "like" the Law School Admission Game and join the Play Like a Law School Expert group on Facebook for regular updates about law school-related news. Ann personally answers law school admission-related questions on her blog at www.lawschoolexpert.com/blog.